Dr. Becca's experience, qualifications, and reputation have established her as a leading voice in helping victims of sexual abuse and exploitation. Her trauma trainings and workshops have impacted thousands of lives across the United States and around the world.
  -- Jeremy Vallerand, CEO, Rescue:Freedom International

Dr. Becca Johnson is a leading psychologist in a field that deals with overcoming trauma. Her easy-to-understand analogies have helped us all better understand the why and how of overcoming our past and giving us tools to go after our futures.
  -- Rebecca Bender, CEO, Rebecca Bender Initiative

Having worked with Dr. Johnson, I know first-hand the expertise, knowledge and compassion she brings to bear. Dr. Johnson developed the trauma therapy program that we use for survivors of sex trafficking.
  -- Lea Newcomb, Executive Director, Engedi Refuge

What others have shared:
Thanks for doing what you do to help people who went through things like me. Once and a thousand times THANK YOU!!!

Dr. Becca's information has sparked a self-reflection in me and made a connection to things in my life that I think have been a problem. I've realized I need to begin taking steps towards healing.

Dr. Johnson brings 25 years of experience as a licensed psychologist as well as a passion to "help the hurting heal". Dr. Becca has focused on helping victims of sexual abuse and exploitation. Becca has served as trainer, counselor, director, consulting psychologist, clinical director and aftercare director for numerous child abuse and anti-trafficking organizations.

The Journey to Hope

OVERCOMING ABUSE

Becca C. Johnson, Ph.D.

Published by Rescue:Freedom International in 2018
ISBN: 0998980005
ISBN 13: 9780998980003

The information contained herein is not intended to be psychotherapy or to substitute for consultation with a licensed health or mental health professional. Application of the contents is at the reader's sole discretion.

This book is dedicated to the many—far too many—who have been abused. May it help with your healing. This book is also dedicated to those who have faced the past and now pursue the future. May you inspire others by your courage and perseverance. Finally, this book is dedicated to those who have shared their stories with me, several for the first time. I am humbled at your trust and rejoice in your renewed power over the pain of your past. May this book be a catalyst for healing.

Contents

Acknowledgments · · · · · · · · · · · · · · · · · · ·xi

Introduction
Who Should Read This Book · · · · · · · xiii

About This Book · · · · · · · · · · · · · · · · ·xix

The Beginning · 1

1   The Journey to Hope? · · · · · · · · · · · · · · · · · · 3

2   Understanding How Healing Happens · · · · · · · · 15

3   What Is Abuse? · 23

4   What We Believed · 35

The Abuse · 43

5   Who Is Abused, How Much, and How Often? · · · 45

6   Who Abuses? · 52

7   Where Abuse Happens · · · · · · · · · · · · · · · · · · 64

The Reactions, Responses, Thoughts, and Feelings · · · 69

8   How Our Bodies React · · · · · · · · · · · · · · · · · 71

9   How Our Minds React · · · · · · · · · · · · · · · · · 76

10   What We Were Told · · · · · · · · · · · · · · · · · · · 82

11   Why We Keep Silent · · · · · · · · · · · · · · · · · · · 88

12   How We Feel · 96

13   Where We Direct the Anger · · · · · · · · · · · · · 107

14   What We Think · 111

15   How We Respond: Symptoms and Behaviors · · · 117

16   What We Did · 125

The Ongoing Challenges · 131

17   How We Feel about the Abuser · · · · · · · · · · · 133

18   What About Forgiveness? · · · · · · · · · · · · · · · 138

19 What Lingers About the Abuse:
      Memories and Triggers · · · · · · · · · · · 145

20 What Helps and What Hinders Our Healing· · · 152

21 What About the Future? · · · · · · · · · · · · · · · 160

22 Future Possibilities and Pursuits · · · · · · · · · · 165

The Healing Story · 171

23 Telling My Abuse Story· · · · · · · · · · · · · · · · · 173

24 Sharing with a Safe Person · · · · · · · · · · · · · 182

25 What's Next · 186

      About the Author· · · · · · · · · · · · · · · · · 189

      Appendix A Possible Indicators of Abuse · · ·191

      Appendix B Letter to the Abuser· · · · · · · · 197

      *Appendix C Letter to a
      Non-offending Caregiver* · · · · · · · · · · · · ·199

      Endnotes · 201

Acknowledgments

I am truly thankful to my supportive husband and family for allowing me to pursue my passion to help the hurting heal.

For the many who have come alongside me on this journey of encouraging the wounded to seek help and healing, I am very appreciative.

To the many survivors who have shared their lives and stories, given feedback, and helped with my own learning, my gratitude overflows.

INTRODUCTION

Who Should Read This Book

I f you have been hurt, hit, used, abused, ignored, denied, threatened, controlled, belittled, and/or shamed, this book was written for you. You have been betrayed, blamed, confused, accused, terrified, and/or tormented. You have experienced physical, sexual, and emotional abuse and neglect. My hope is that, by reading and then choosing to complete the questions and checklists, you will move from abuse to hope and healing. The road is not always easy, but the destination is worth the time, energy, and effort.

This book should also be read by family, friends, and professional counselors who want to gain more knowledge, understanding, and empathy. I strongly believe that without heart and understanding (empathy), knowledge alone is ineffective in helping others. In reading this book, support people will gain a heart and mind perspective needed to assist the abused friend, family member, or client.

This book was written to be informal, inviting, and easy to read. While it is filled with factual information about the trauma of abuse, I've woven a few stories into the chapters, along with checklists and fill-in-the-blank statements.

You are invited to join in the journey to learn about abuse, heal from abuse, or help others on the journey of healing from abuse.

To summarize, the goals of this book are to help readers:

1. To learn
    - It is for *those who have been abused* and want to learn about it, but do not yet want to face it head on.
    - It is for *those not sure if they were abused* and want to learn about it, wondering if what happened would be considered abuse.
    - It is also for *anyone* who wants to learn about abuse, whether for gaining knowledge or seeking answers.
2. To heal
    - It is also for *victims* of abuse who want to heal and deal directly with what happened to them—those who want to begin or continue their journey to emotional health.
3. To help
    - This book is also for those *family, friends, or therapists* who want to help by gaining knowledge

and by giving this workbook to others to assist the abused.

For Those of You Looking at Your Abuse for the First Time

For those facing abuse for the first time, or those unsure whether what happened would be considered abuse, I encourage you to approach this as if it were a school textbook filled with lots of facts and information. Your goal is to learn about abuse and trauma, not deal with them personally—until you are ready. Though your mind will likely take you to what happened in your past, I would encourage you to try to keep this as a learning exercise. Instead of completing the checklists, just read them. Your safety is of utmost concern.

Healing from trauma includes facing painful memories, powerful feelings, and potentially harmful behaviors. To do this, you need to feel emotionally and physically safe, and you need to have supportive and safe people around you: family, friends, a support group, and/or a professional therapist. If you don't feel safe, healing won't happen.

If you're not ready, facing the abuse too soon or too quickly might make you feel unsafe and even more apprehensive about addressing it in the future. You might also feel re-traumatized. If the material becomes too overwhelming, set it down, and return to it when you're ready. But do return to it someday. When you feel emotionally safe and have friends, family, and/or a counselor supporting you, reread the book, and complete the checklists.

For Those of You Wanting to Deal With Your Abusive Past

For those ready to face what happened, to heal, and to move on, I encourage you to read the information and complete the checklists and questions. Avoid the pitfall of comparing your experiences with those of others or minimizing what happened to you. Whether once or a multitude of times, whether fondling or rape, whether bruises or broken bones, all abuse is traumatic.

Doing the "My Experience" sections will help you identify, clarify, and express what has probably been stuffed inside for far too long. Using this guide as a workbook aids in your path to health and wholeness.

However, as mentioned in the previous section, do not proceed unless you have assessed your situation and the emotional risks involved. Are you ready? Do you have the strength and safety needed? Do you have a support system in place to help you through the especially tough times? It is good to be stretched and challenged in life, but not broken. You'll need to determine when or if you need to take a break from the material. But do return to finish this recovery road when you feel safe, supported, and ready.

At times, you may feel like you are taking two steps forward, three steps back, but that is part of the journey. Soon, you will be gaining much more than you imagined possible.

For Family, Friends, and Professionals Wanting to Help Those Who Have Been Abused

Family and Friends. Your goal in reading this book is not only to become more knowledgeable about abuse, but more importantly, to become more empathetic and understanding of what your family member or friend may have experienced and what he or she may feel, think, and believe. Your caring, sensitivity, understanding, and empathy can greatly help. You can provide the listening ear and loving response needed to help in the healing of those wounded by abuse.

Therapists and Professionals. You may choose to use this in a variety of ways. Recommending and/or providing the book for individuals seeking help for abuse is key. Or perhaps you'll want to use the book as a guide in therapy, as a workbook to accompany therapy, or as homework for sessions. The overall goal is for the client to complete the workbook, which simultaneously accomplishes the sharing of the trauma narrative—a key in trauma recovery.

About This Book

Some keys about this book and its format are as follows:

- Most chapters are short.
- Each chapter generally begins with a bit of information or facts, not a lot.
- I've tried to include stories to illustrate topics and make the material more interesting, applicable, and readable.
- Italicized sentences represent statements, made to me by victims, that I've tried to remember over the years. The words accurately reflect thoughts, feelings, sentiments, and events, even if not relayed verbatim.
- If names are used they are pseudonyms for actual names, used to protect confidentiality.
- Though the abused are both male and female, I more frequently refer to victims as female due to my experience working primarily with girls and women, the fact that more women experience abuse than men, as well as out of habit.

- Each chapter includes "My Experience," a section that encourages specific recollections of your abuse. Again, do not do these unless you feel emotionally ready, safe, and supported. Some readers will check a few items, while others will check many. It depends on your experience and what happened to you.

- Please don't compare yourself to others or minimize your experience based on the number of items you do or don't check. All is trauma—whether once or a thousand times; whether after disobedience or compliance; whether rape or fondling; and whether slapped, whipped, or kicked. The extensive checklists are to include the breadth of experiences, not necessarily the depth. That is, the lists seek to include something from each person's experiences, not imply that the items listed represent everything an abused person normally encounters. Different people will mark different answers, according to their different experiences.

- Lastly, space is provided for "Reflections"—for you to write, draw, or doodle as you please. Use these blank pages to express rather than repress, and spew rather than stuff, whether expressing emotions, thoughts, or confusion.

The Beginning

If you can't fly then run, if you can't run then walk, if you can't walk then crawl, but whatever you do you have to keep moving forward.
—MARTIN LUTHER KING, JR.

CHAPTER 1

The Journey to Hope?

The word *journey* implies movement and a destination. We are heading somewhere, moving toward a chosen goal. There may be challenges and mishaps, but the destination is desired.

That's what this book is about: moving in a desired direction, the desire to heal from abuse. This is an important, much-needed journey. The destination is a place of freedom and hope. You may not wholeheartedly desire this exploration, but you know, somewhere in the deep realms of your heart or the hidden places in your mind, that the destination is worth the blood, sweat, and tears of the trek.

While most books on abuse focus on the journey of healing, the focus here is on the entire journey: the journey into, within, and out of abuse; the before, during, and after; the good, bad, ugly, and uglier; the pre and post; the who, what, why, when, and where.

No one chooses to be on this abuse journey. We would rather rewrite our pasts and exclude those people, places, and events that hint at or haunt us with memories of abuse. We wish we weren't on this path.

The journey of abuse is unique. Your story is different from your friend's, from your neighbor's, from your sister's, from your mother's, from your uncle's, from your grandfather's, or from your teacher's. It is yours and yours alone. You may describe your experience as challenging, overwhelming, or all consuming; painful, excruciating, or hell; dismissed or denied; unforgettable or unforgivable; horrible or haunting; silent, secret, and/or shameful. Or maybe there still aren't words to adequately express and explain what happened to you.

No two journeys are exactly alike, although there may be similarities.

A Common Journey

Though your abuse journey is unique, there are some common routes. One could be summarized in the following, all too simplified example. The order of the steps varies from person to person, but generally includes many of the following aspects:

- A minor is abused (physical, sexual, and/or emotional abuse, or neglect), or an adult is assaulted (physical, sexual, emotional).
- The person (victim) feels confused and, more often than not, doesn't tell anyone.
- The person blames himself or herself.

- The person feels different, self-hatred, stupid, shame, fear (of others knowing), and/or anger (primarily directed at self).
- The person attempts to deny, repress, ignore, rationalize, recant, dissociate, or minimize the trauma or abuse.
- The person usually does not think of himself or herself as a victim.
- The person may internalize or externalize symptoms of trauma.
- The person exhibits emotional, behavioral, or physiological problems and concerns.
- The person may be tested, evaluated, labeled, or diagnosed.
- The person may be re-victimized (at any point in this process).
- The person generally does not get help nor want to address the symptoms, impact, effect, emotions, and/ or negative self-thoughts of the abuse.
- The person lives with internalized, negative thoughts and feelings and lives below his or her potential.

Did this overly simplified route seem similar to yours? Did you feel that it somewhat summarized your own life experience? Or did you think to yourself, "That's not at all like what I experienced"? This is just one example of the many routes taken by those who have been abused.

Below, the journey is summarized and simplified again. It is the most-traveled journey for the abused.

Transition to Tragedy *(Becca C. Johnson, 2015)*

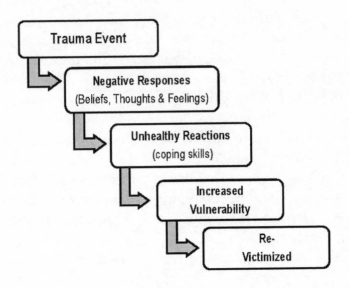

This journey isn't over. Reaching hope is definitely possible. You need to continue toward this destination: a journey to hope. Don't stop short, but continue and cross the finish line to healing.

Is Healing Possible?

Some have asked, "Is healing even possible?" To that, I must admit that I've had times of doubt. I've worked directly with some victims who have been so multiply abused and exploited that I have doubted the possibility of restoration. The emotional effects of the abuse, assaults, and exploitation seemed insurmountable.

I remember how my own doubts grew as I worked with a particular young lady who had been abused not once, not twice, but by three different people over the course of seven years, from ages six to thirteen. When she came in for counseling, she had an eating disorder, was engaged in self-harm cutting behaviors, and was also self-medicating—using drugs to deaden the inner pain and shame.

She was depressed, angry (at herself), shut down, and resistant, and she conveyed a sense of hopelessness. As a counselor, I'm supposed to rise above the client's emotional state; with her, I found that I too felt a sense of hopelessness. I was overwhelmed by the depth of her hurt and pain. It was difficult to see change as possible and to believe hope was a reality.

As our sessions progressed, however, she began to open up. Little by little, she shared her vulnerable thoughts and feelings, as well as her dreadful doubts. Eventually, she vomited the horrors of her past and slowly regained strength.

Soon, she was no longer cutting herself and even stopped her drug use. She gained control over her eating habits and after a long drought of happiness, she began to smile again.

As my doubts subsided, hope increased. I wondered how I could ever have doubted the power of human resilience. How could I have forgotten the incredible capacity and overwhelming force of hope? I was a believer again in the ability to overcome severe adversity, to face both hardship and trauma in the boxing ring, and to emerge victorious.

In the midst of despair, it can be difficult to see the possibility of restoration. Amid your traumas, pain, and shame, it can be challenging to believe that healing is attainable.

ACE: Adverse Childhood Experiences

Adverse childhood experiences (ACEs) are child abuse, negative experiences, and trauma. A list of ACEs was compiled that included all forms of child abuse, neglect, domestic violence, caregiver substance abuse, incarceration, and mental illness. Thousands of people were asked to indicate how many of these traumas they had experienced while growing up. Additional information was then gathered about each person's life history, including health problems, life choices, habits, relationships, and more.

The study revealed that it is not uncommon to have at least one of the ACEs, and that two out of three people do. More than 20 percent—or one in five people—have three ACEs or more. To simplify and summarize the results, the higher your ACE score (or the more childhood traumatic experiences you have faced), the greater the likelihood that you will experience physical and mental health problems, and negative social consequences, later in life. You are at greater risk of developing the following:

- Alcohol and substance abuse
- Heart and liver problems
- Depression
- Health-related quality of life
- Poor work performance
- Financial stress
- Risk of domestic and sexual violence
- Multiple sexual partners
- Sexually transmitted diseases
- Smoking habit
- Suicide attempts

- Unintended pregnancies
- Early initiation of sex and teenage pregnancy
- Poor school performance

For more information on the ACE study, refer to the U.S. Center for Disease Control and Prevention.

Childhood traumas are internalized and yet manifest themselves externally in relationship and work problems, health and mental health issues, harmful habits, substance abuse, and more. The problem is that most people who have been traumatized are not given help in dealing with the traumas, don't know where to get help or don't pursue the help or healing needed. When you seek help and face your past—rather than run from it—these risk factors lessen, and your quality of life improves. Why continue to live in a state of emotional turmoil, denial, and increased problems? It's better to work through it rather than around it—for improved overall emotional and physical well-being.

The Courage to Hope

When Mira came to counseling, she boldly declared her desire to "finally deal with the abuse I experienced as a child." She sounded determined to face her trauma during that first session. Subsequent meetings, however, proved that her resolve was not as strong as it first appeared. Session after session she focused on unrelated annoyances in her current life situation and avoided any mention of the abuse. It seemed too insurmountable for her to climb, too scary to face, and too overwhelming to conquer. She retreated before beginning; she surrendered before the fight began.

Your healing journey will at times feel like a fight. You'll want to surrender and say it's not worth it. You'll want to give in when the going gets tough. But I encourage you to confront the painful past and maintain course, to keep on keeping on, to hang in there even when the journey seems daunting and demanding. It will make a difference in your life—for the better. You will be free of that pit in your stomach, the bitterness in your heart, the catch in your throat, and the self-hating thoughts in your mind.

This book is titled *The Journey to Hope* because that's what I believe. As you venture down this path, the destination is hope and healing, restoration and rejoicing.

The Journey of Healing

Let's take another look at the journey outlined above. Let's interpose new facts and redirect the route:

- The person realizes the need to address the symptoms, impact, negative emotions, and false thinking of the trauma or abuse.
- The person gets or seeks support and help and begins addressing the effects of the abuse on his or her life.
- The person experiences renewed freedom from the pain, renewed hope, and healing.

Most would choose *this* journey to hope over stagnating in the negative effects of abuse, yet, unfortunately, many don't choose this route. Please don't run from what happened to you, minimize its effects, or ignore it. When you're ready, face and address it. When it's painful, persevere. When it's challenging, continue on. When you want to quit, commit to stay.

The Importance of Emotional Healing and the Dynamics of Recidivism/Revictimization

Practical needs *without* emotional healing: High risk of revictimization and a shame-filled life

Practical needs *plus* emotional healing: Restoration and a hope-filled life

(Becca C. Johnson, 2008)

Without emotional healing, you are much more vulnerable to being revictimized. Without healing, you are more likely to continue to live buried in shame and self-blame. With emotional healing, you can experience freedom from the painful past, and hope can be restored.

Hope is believing there is a light at the end of the long, dark tunnel. It is the defiant, stubborn, hope-filled flower that sprouts amid the cold, harsh winter snow. Hope revives the soul and brings possibility where none existed before. To a deadened soul, hope is breath giving and life restoring.

The courage to hope is a journey of healing from abuse.

Many years ago, I lived next to a large county park that was used primarily by joggers and hikers. At the entry gate was a sign informing park users of inherent dangers. A large poster warned of mountain lions in the area and provided instructions on what to do if you encountered this large, wild animal. One day, I read an article in the local newspaper about a jogger who was chased by a mountain lion. Fortunately, he remembered the instructions. He stopped, turned, and faced the mountain lion! Now, that goes against our natural instincts and takes a lot of courage. Yet in response, the animal stopped, then walked away.

That's what is needed in healing from trauma and abuse. Turn and face it, rather than run from it. Rather than ignore, pretend, minimize, or hide, we must address the feelings, thoughts, lies, defenses, anger, and unhelpful behaviors. We must shed any self-sabotaging habits once and for all. As we turn and face our painful pasts, we gain strength and control. And like the mountain lion, the pain ceases and departs, leaving us with more peace and joy in our lives.

Choosing to join the journey to address the abuse is the first step toward a wonderfully desirable destination. Please join this excursion. Don't deny or delay.

The next chapter summarizes the components of the healing process before we begin the who, what, when, and where of abuse.

My Experience
(Check as many as apply.)

___ I'm not yet ready to dive in and address my past abuse head on, but will be open to it in the future.

___ For now, I'll read the material but won't complete the checklists.

___ My journey has been somewhat similar to the example given above.

___ I'm ready to face my past, the abuse, and what came with it.

Reflections

Thoughts, feelings, drawings, notes, or doodles

CHAPTER 2

Understanding How Healing Happens

t's been my privilege for the past twenty-five years, to work with many who have been abused. They have bravely faced their deep shame, dark fears, misplaced self-anger, and unjustified self-hatred. They've learned to shed these uninvited intruders with courage and grace. But it wasn't always easy. The telling of one's trauma experiences is like bitter medicine—bad tasting, but good for you and important in your recovery.

I don't want to lose you with this chapter. We're not ready to begin this path toward healing just yet. First, I'd like to talk about how the healing process works and what's involved. Perhaps I could summarize this chapter by saying that woven within the pages of this book are many of the steps considered essential in trauma recovery, *and this understanding will help you navigate through this book.* The information and checklists take you on an intentional journey. This isn't just a series of fact-finding chapters aimed at evoking painful memories. Instead, this manuscript has a clear, focused purpose—to lead you on a healing adventure. I chose the word *adventure* here because it connotes some possible danger and excitement—or at least some emotional experiences that you will have. Simply put, this book intentionally incorporates key components, deemed by research and experience, to be helpful for healing. The rest of this chapter explains these key components and includes some information I think is interesting.

Both from my personal and professional experience, as well as from reading and studying, I know that sharing your trauma story is key in the healing process. You are encouraged to get it out rather than let it fester inside like a cancerous growth infecting the soul and robbing you of future hope. The unspeakable needs to be spoken.

The telling of your abuse history, however, is easier said than done. Revisiting what happened is the last thing you want to do. Many find this necessary healing task to be excruciatingly painful, even in the confidentiality of a counseling office.

Not long ago, I led a support group for victims of physical and sexual abuse. I informed everyone that our last two sessions would be devoted to telling our stories. Though optional, I encouraged everyone to share, knowing the healing power of sharing one's narrative. When it came time, few chose to share. I then took out some checklists I'd compiled (now in this book), asking the group to fill them out. When they finished, I asked again if anyone wanted to share. Everyone did.

I didn't expect such a response. Those brave people became even more courageous with the help of the checklists. They didn't have to explain or expound, find the words, or give the gory details. The checklists did that for them. The lists about the who, what, when, and where of abuse made sharing one's story both safer and easier!

I am hoping that you, too, will find the task of working through and sharing your story not as daunting as first imagined. This book, with its checklists and questions, enables you to tell your story without also requiring you to know or have the words needed to explain what happened. The lists (which include the people, places, events, thoughts, feelings, and more) enhance recollections and facilitate healing, making the task of getting it out easier.

One abuse survivor shared,

When I was asked to tell what happened, my mind went blank. But when I used the checklists, it was as if someone were reading my mind and knew exactly what I was thinking and feeling—even when I didn't have words to express or explain it myself.

The checklists in this book have given a voice to numerous victims who were previously unable or unwilling to speak out and tell their stories. The checklists have helped many, some for the first time, to examine their trauma and better understand what happened.

Interesting to Know—Components of the Healing Process

In addition to sharing your story of abuse, there are other important steps to take in this journey of healing.

It's important that…

- You have a sense of *safety* as you address the trauma. You shouldn't feel pushed, prodded, or pressured to deal with the painful past until, and unless, you have a sense of emotional, as well as physical safety.
- You understand and learn more about trauma and abuse. *Educate* yourself and learn from others— what abuse is; when, where, and how it happens; how people react; who is affected; and how it affects a victim's thinking, emotions, and behaviors. Learning about abuse and trauma helps you to realize, sometimes for the first time, that you are not alone nor are you "crazy." (This is referred to as *psychoeducation,* sort of like educating yourself about the psychological effects of abuse and trauma.)
- You learn and use *relaxation* skills, identifying and implementing what helps you calm yourself. These are needed when trauma memories are anxiety producing or trigger flashbacks. Some may refer to this healing step as anxiety management, stress reduction, grounding, or positive self-soothing, among other terms.
- You continually strive for *emotional health.* Trauma victims' emotions often become heightened, blunted, overwhelmed, numbed, unpredictable,

inconsistent, and/or out-of-proportion, and need to be realigned. (This is also referred to as emotional or affective regulation.) An important part of healing is learning or relearning about your feelings and emotional responses.

- You correct *wrong thinking.* You are encouraged to identify and correct false or unhelpful thoughts that have formed the foundation of your beliefs and attitudes about the world, others, and yourself. (This is also referred to as cognitive distortion, false thinking, or negative self-talk.) I prefer to refer to these as the lies we believe resulting from having been abused, traumatized, and exploited.

- You *tell your story and get it out.* Like surgery when removing a cancerous growth, you are urged to let it out rather than let it fester inside—but in your own time, when you are ready and feel safe. (This is also known as the trauma narrative.)

- You regain *future hope,* which is the capstone of moving on. You are encouraged to put the abuse in perspective as part of your life story, not allowing it to define you or your identity, or to determine your future. Self-chosen goals, dreams, and plans are rekindled and revisited. (This combines various aspects of what is referred to as promoting resiliency, problem solving, future planning, and/or fostering self-efficacy.) Basically, as you heal and regain or renew a sense of who you are, your dreams and hopes return. The abuse is but one chapter in your life, not the entire book, nor the end of the story.

This list was developed from various sources identifying components of trauma treatment across trauma treatment modalities (refer to references at the end of the book). [1]

These components of trauma healing are intentionally woven into the chapters of this book and facilitate your healing journey.

How?

This book facilitates healing by incorporating the key elements of trauma recovery listed above. Methods for accomplishing this goal include the following:

- It allows you to determine your level of *safety* or involvement, whether to read the book for learning or to dive in by completing the various checklists and questions.
- It *educates*, providing much information about abuse and trauma.
- It encourages the acknowledgment, identification, and transparency of *emotions*.
- It exposes the *wrong thinking* all too common for those affected by abuse.
- It fosters the use of *relaxation* skills and other activities helpful to the healing process.
- And all the while, those choosing to complete the "My Experience" section, with its checklists and questions, are pulling together all of the helpful parts for *telling your story*.
- Lastly, before finishing, you are invited to identify any residual or leftover memories and triggers,

as well as current thoughts, feelings, dreams, and plans—all focused on increasing healing and instilling *future hope.*

Seeking a Professional Counselor

This journey is not meant to be taken alone, though you alone must work through the lies, feelings, reactions, and results of what happened to you. It is best taken with a close friend or family member by your side to provide a listening ear and a comforting shoulder, and/or a professional counselor who can help guide as well as provide valuable insight.

When seeking a counselor, it is important to know that sometimes it takes a while to find the right one. It's like any relationship. With some people, you feel comfortable, and yet with others, the relationship just never seems to get off the ground. Do not blame yourself, and don't give up. It's just not a match. Ask for a recommendation or call a local mental health center.

When "interviewing" the counselor, be sure to ask if the counselor has experience working with victims of childhood trauma. And you decide whether you want to see a male or a female therapist. Some accept insurance, some have fixed rates, and others offer a sliding scale or fee based on income level. Some communities have counseling centers that offer services at a reduced rate.

If at any time you feel uncomfortable or misunderstood, don't drop out. Return to discuss your concern. I've found that counseling sessions improve and healing increases after someone has bravely shared a concern with me—whether something I said or did. It helps me become more aware and more sensitive, and helps sessions become more beneficial.

CHAPTER 3

What Is Abuse?

A child generally doesn't know what is or isn't abuse. It can be confusing or vague. Many who have been abused didn't know that what they experienced would be considered abuse.

I remember a young woman who shared with me about a relationship she'd regretted when she was younger. She was about thirteen years old at the time. A college student, tutoring a group of middle schoolers, made unwanted sexual advances and then coerced her into having sex. She said she'd never told anyone before and that ever since that happened, she felt a lot of shame about it. After she shared, I turned to her and said, "Did you know that what happened to you was abuse? It is considered child abuse."

She looked at me in shock as my words began to sink in. "No, really? What? Are you sure?"

Fortunately, that disclosure began her journey of healing. She was able to remove the shame and regret in her life.

This book is written for those of you who have suffered any type of abuse, whether physical, emotional, sexual, or neglect. Although my experience as a psychologist has primarily focused on sexual abuse and exploitation, it is seldom that I meet those who were sexually abused who were not also physically and/or emotionally abused, or those who were primarily physically abused, but were also in some way shamed sexually and verbally.

Sexual Abuse

Sexual abuse encompasses a wide variety of inappropriate behaviors and activities that can happen both directly and indirectly. One study revealed that over one in three women experienced a direct form of sexual abuse before age eighteen. When the definition was broadened to include indirect (noncontact) sexual activities, 54 percent of the women reported having been sexually abused as a minor. That's one in two women, or every other woman!

Indirect: Sexual activities that do not involve direct contact with the offender, yet are undesired and considered abuse, include indecent exposure; an adult or older child engaging in voyeurism (observing the minor undress, bathe, urinate, etc.); child pornography (photographing nudity of or having a minor engage in explicit acts); and allowing, showing, or forcing a minor to watch pornography or other sexual activities (i.e., someone masturbating, sex, or an orgy).

I had to parade around nude and dance while he watched.

They took pictures of me sitting with my legs apart.

My mom and her partner would have sex in front of me and tell me to watch.

(Italicized quotes throughout the book represent statements or sentiments made by those who have been abused.)

Direct: Sexual abuse also includes any sexual activity that involves contact with the perpetrator. It can include fondling, rubbing, and sitting on a lap, digital (finger) and penile penetration (vaginal or anal), oral sex, bestiality (sex with animals), as well as various forms or versions of these. Orgies, sexual bondage and discipline (B and D), dominance and submission (D/s), sadism and masochism (S and M), multiple-entry sex (combination of sexual activities), and ritualistic abuse are also among the many abusive activities.

I had to sit on his lap and move back and forth until he finished his business.

He raped me every Thursday night when my mom was at her women's group.

She'd get into bed with me, and we'd touch each other's private parts.

Physical Abuse

When someone inflicts bodily harm that results in a physical injury to another person, this is physical abuse.

Visible injuries include bruises, burns, black eyes, and cuts. Some physical injuries, however, are not visible. Internal injuries, head trauma, and broken bones resulting from an abusive encounter may not be seen. Some victims have shared of being burned by cigarettes on their feet or hit on the head with a bottle, places where the marks of the injury are not easily seen.

Physical abuse includes hitting, kicking, pushing, shoving, beating, whipping, slapping, punching, throwing, burning, exposure, withholding daily needs, severe punishment, and more—anything that results in physical injury, intentional deprivation, and/or harm. I have heard of young children being immersed in boiling water and of others forced to stay barefoot outside in the snow.

Physical abuse goes far beyond constructive discipline. It steps over the line. While some parental punishment is harsh and abusive, other caregiver conduct may be strict, but not considered abuse. When in doubt, parents, don't do it. Constructive discipline and positive reinforcement are far better and healthier means of training and guiding children.

> *I had my head dunked in the toilet by my stepdad when I got in trouble.*
>
> *My hand was put over the stove burner when my mom got mad.*
>
> *My dad spanked me so hard with the wooden spoon that I couldn't sit down for days.*
>
> *If I did something wrong I'd be kept in a closet all day, with no food or water, and I wasn't even allowed to go to the bathroom. Then, I'd get a beating if I wet myself.*

Neglect

Neglect occurs when caregivers fail to provide for the child or adolescent. Most reports of neglect involve lack of proper food, shelter, clothing, medical care, and supervision. While a majority of neglect is the result of caregiver addictions, some is the result of ignorance of proper childcare. There is also some neglect, though hard to imagine, that involves the deliberate maltreatment of the minor. Neglect happens in all economic levels, not just those with limited resources. Drug-dependent caregivers, mentally ill parents, busy professionals, and others have neglected the needs of their children. While most cases reflect the lack of meeting the physical needs of the child, the emotional needs of the child may also be ignored. The neglect of proper nurturing, love, and attachment are more challenging for the victim to overcome than lack of food, clothing, or shelter.

> *My parents were so strung out on drugs, they didn't take care of my sister and me. We were left with no food and had to fend for ourselves. We'd go through the neighbors' garbage trying to find food.*
>
> *My mom worked two jobs and was gone most of the time. We were pretty much left on our own. Most days we'd come home from school, get some food, watch TV, and put ourselves to bed.*

Emotional Abuse

Emotional abuse is also known as verbal, psychological, or mental abuse. What one person might consider abusive, another might label as poor parenting or excuse as the results of a "dysfunctional family." It may be defined as any act or lack of action that endangers the mental health and emotional development of a minor. This may include degradation and ridicule, such as continual insults, belittling, and threats, and/or the exposure of the child to violence within the home, such as domestic violence. Emotional abuse includes situations where children are put in the middle of divorce disputes or relationship breakdowns. These children are used by a parent to vent about the partner (forcing the child into the emotionally difficult position of having to "choose"). Emotional abuse also occurs when the minor is used for the emotional support and as a listening ear for a parent or adult. Some refer to this as emotional incest.

I think I was called almost every name in the book—stupid, ugly, worthless, incompetent, good-for-nothing, and a lot of other words I wouldn't want to say out loud.

I tried not to let what they'd say get to me, but what hurt the most was when they'd say, "I wished you'd never been born." That still hurts.

I was terrified when my parents got into a fight. When I tried to stop the violence, I got hurt, so I stopped trying, but I kept wishing it would end.

My mom used to sit on my bed and tell me how much she hated dad and all about their sex life. She'd talk about how he was worthless, couldn't get it up all the time, and didn't provide the things she wanted in life. I wanted to scream and tell her to shut up,

*but I knew I couldn't. Mom needed me. I was afraid
she'd fall apart and leave me, too. Looking back now
as an adult, I realize that I felt like her therapist.*

Multiple Abuses

Unfortunately, many, if not most, victims of abuse experience more than one type of abuse. One woman shared that she had experienced physical, verbal, and emotional abuse from both of her parents, as well as sexual abuse from older siblings. She was told that she was worthless and stupid, and was often forced to hand wash the family's laundry, then physically abused if it "wasn't done right." Her parents and other family members referred to her as "the witch" and "the devil's daughter" (physical, sexual, psychological abuse).

> *I would be raped and then beaten and told that it was
> my fault for what he did.* (sexual, physical, verbal
> abuse)
> *While being kicked, I'd be told that I was dirty, smelly
> crap.* (physical, verbal abuse)

Reminder: Do not do "My Experience" unless you feel emotionally ready, safe, and supported. You can always skip this section and come back later. Please don't compare yourself to others or minimize your experience based on the number you do or don't check. You may check a few items or many. It depends on your experience and what happened to you. All is abuse, all is trauma.

My Experience

Check those events that happened to you on the following lists, marking as many as apply. If what happened to you is not listed, add it to the list under "Other." (A thorough list of possible indicators of abuse is included in Appendix A.)

Sexual Abuse:

___ Fondling or touching
___ Penile penetration (vagina), intercourse
___ Sodomy (anal sex)
___ Sexual violence (forced touching, sex act, etc.)
___ Voyeurism (being watched during bathing, dressing, urination, etc.)
___ Indecent exposure (other showing his or her private parts)
___ Object or finger penetration (into vagina or anus)
___ Oral sex (done on you or by you; cunnilingus or fellatio)
___ Pornography (allowed, encouraged, or forced to watch)
___ Pornography (photos or videos taken of you nude or scantily clad)
___ Pornography (being filmed while doing sexual activities)
___ Being given to others for sexual activities
___ Being sold to others for sex (prostituted)
___ Encouraged or forced to provide sexual activities in exchange for basic needs (food, clothing, shelter, money; survival sex)

___ Masturbation (watching or doing on self or others)
___ Sexual activities with animals (bestiality)
___ Parading or dancing around (nude or few clothes)
___ Ritual abuse involving sexual activities
___ Forced to partake in multiple-member sex orgies
___ Any sexual activity done by a family member
___ Other:_____
___ Other:_____

Physical Abuse:

___ Kicked
___ Beat, hit, shoved, pushed, slapped, thrown
___ Cut, bitten, punctured, stabbed
___ Trapped, smothered
___ Closeted (for several hours, several days, or long amounts of time)
___ Burned
___ Whipped, slashed
___ Exposure to elements (sun, wind, cold, or storms) without proper clothing or gear
___ Other:_____

Resulting in:

___ Stitches
___ Fractures
___ Dislocations
___ Bruises, black eye, welts
___ Bleeding

___ Difficulty with daily physical activities: walking, sitting, running, standing
___ Lacerations and cuts
___ Need for medication
___ Need for bandaging
___ Emergency room visit
___ Doctor's visit
___ Other: _____

Neglect:

___ Lack of food
___ Lack of clothing
___ Lack of shelter (safe place to stay and sleep)
___ Lack of nurturance (love, affection, bonding)
___ Lack of medical care
___ Lack of proper supervision
___ Other: _____

Emotional Abuse:

___ Degradation, belittling, ridicule, insults
___ Verbal threats
___ Witnessing family violence
___ Put in the middle of parental disputes and/or forced to take sides
___ Used by an adult to vent inappropriate content and/or emotions
___ Depended upon as an adult's emotional support

___ Continual, intentional withholding of emotional support (ignoring or silent treatment as punishment)
___ Other: _____

Check the statements below that apply to you, then write about any thoughts or feelings you may have.

___ It's hard to think about what happened.
___ I wish I could forget what happened.
___ This is hard to deal with, but I'm not going to run away from facing it.
___ I'll face it but I'm going to take it slowly.
___ Other: _____

Reflections

Thoughts, feelings, drawings, notes, or doodles

CHAPTER 4

What We Believed

Whether you are aware of it or not, you've developed beliefs about abuse from your communities, society, the media, and from those around you. Many—if not most—of these beliefs are unhealthy.

You Believed That Abuse Was Rare

It wasn't long ago that people believed there to be few cases of child abuse. In the mid-1950s, it was believed that only one in one thousand children experienced it. As time progressed, the belief increased to one in one hundred children. Even now, there are some who contend that media information is exaggerating or that victims are pity seekers. Now, we know better. The reality is: It happens. It's prevalent. It cannot be ignored or minimized.

You Believed That Certain Acts Weren't Abuse

Whenever I've defined and explained what is and isn't abuse, whether in counseling or training, there are usually people who have realized for the first time that what happened to them *was* abuse. All too often, harmful and abusive behaviors are mislabeled, minimized, or misidentified.

Perhaps you grew up, as many do, unsure about what is and isn't abuse. Some might say,

> *He was just overly affectionate.*
> *That's just Uncle Tim's way of playing.*
> *It was strict discipline.*
> *Though I experienced it a lot, I wasn't touched, so it's not abuse.*

You Believed That You Were Not Supposed to Tell

Too many people have been raised in families, cultures, or communities that have minimized abuse and its negative impact on the abused. Maybe you heard statements (whether actually said aloud or implied) like these:

> *Get over it.*
> *Just ignore it.*
> *That's just the way it is.*
> *Men are like that.*
> *Don't say anything. We don't want the family* to get a bad name.*

*Don't tell because it would be too shameful or would
ruin us.**
(*abuser, community, club, church, school, business, etc.)

In one community, it was assumed that victims
must suck it up because exposure of the truth of
abuse would tarnish the community's image,
which was viewed as vastly more important than
what happened to the individual. In fact, victims are
placed in a room with the abuser and told to forgive,
for the good of the community. I cringe at this
response, believing it to be re-victimizing.

You clearly understood that it was best not to tell because you wouldn't be heard or believed—your feelings
and what happened would be minimized or ignored.

Victims become the sacrificial lamb for what others
consider the greater good. Yet we now know that, in most
cases, the victimization continues (the abuser continues
to abuse, finding more victims), and those falling prey
are left with the overwhelming challenge of healing—
generally alone and without a supportive, healing family
or community.

You Believed That You Would Be Blamed

You've read about or experienced victim blaming. "It
was her fault for wearing *those* clothes" (skimpy, provoca-
tive, sensuous, scantily clad). The victim is blamed rather
than the victimizer.

One young girl of six was being abused by a teenage cousin. When a parent walked in on the sexual abuse, *both* were scolded for doing "such a terrible thing." The parent didn't differentiate between victim and victimizer but blamed both.

Many don't tell what happened to them due to this fear of being blamed and the shame that accompanies it. So they end up believing that it is best not to say anything, to keep quiet, and to do what they've heard or understood: "Get over it" or "just ignore it."

One survivor shared that she was not able to wear cool clothes like her peers because it would arouse her stepdad. She was told that the abuse was her fault for "being so cute and dressing so sexy."

You Believed That If You Did Speak Out about Abuse, Nothing Would Happen or Change

Not only do many victims get blamed, they also get ignored. Many believe that if a victim tells, nothing will be done to help or to stop the abuse. Their cries for help will go unnoticed or fall on deaf ears.

> *I knew that no one would do anything, so why bother telling?*
> *I felt like no one cared about me, like I'd just be ignored if I said anything about what was going on.*

But the truth is, abuse is a traumatic violation, not a small infraction. Keeping quiet is not good for you.

It changed my life and how I viewed myself and others— for the worse.

I knew that I wasn't supposed to tell because the family might fall apart. He'd go to jail and we wouldn't have any money.

At first, I didn't think it was wrong. I just thought it was something that everybody does.

I believe that, because of the abuse, I started using drugs and became promiscuous.

The abuse taught me that what I think and feel, and what happens to me, doesn't matter.

My Experience

(Check as many as apply)

___ I believed that abuse was rare.

___ I believed that, since abuse is rare, then there must be something wrong with me because it was happening to me.

___ I didn't know that what was going on was abuse.

___ I believed that I wasn't supposed to tell.

___ I believed that I would be blamed.

___ I believed that if I told, no one would do anything about it.

___ Other: _____

Reflections

Thoughts, feelings, drawings, notes, or doodles

The Abuse

"One's dignity may be assaulted,
vandalized and cruelly mocked,
but it can never be taken away
unless it is surrendered."
— MICHAEL J. FOX

CHAPTER 5

Who Is Abused, How Much, and How Often?

One night, as my husband was reading the daily newspaper, he stopped and brought something to my attention. There on the front page were three articles about accusations of child abuse. One of the accused was a famous singer, another a Catholic priest, and the third was a local youth-club leader.

When I was younger and first learned about child abuse, I remember thinking that it didn't happen among devout religious communities. It couldn't. Then I read of spiritual cults using and abusing their members, young and old. I also naively thought that rich people didn't neglect their children. Why would they? How could they? They have the resources to take care of or provide for their children. I had much to learn.

Anyone can be abused. There is no group or family, community or nation that is immune. Abuse happens to those of all races and religions, ages, wages, stages, genders, and generations. Unfortunately, abuse exists and is all too common. Anyone from anywhere can be abused.

To answer the question, "Who is abused?" I reply, "Far too many!"

Statistics

Information on the number of minors that have been or are being abused is inaccurate. Statistics gathered only tell us the number of reports made and not actual incidents of abuse, and we know that the majority go unreported. For example, an estimated 3.4 million referrals involving the alleged maltreatment of approximately 6.3 million children were made to Child Protective Services agencies in the United States in 2012.[2]

This is only the tip of the iceberg. If we were to literally use this analogy and apply iceberg percentages, where 86 percent is underwater, then the number of abused children would be almost thirty-nine million.

Here's more startling data:

1. A report of child abuse is made every ten seconds.
2. Child abuse occurs at every socioeconomic level, across ethnic and cultural lines, within all religions, and at all levels of education.[3]

3. Of those surveyed in a large study in the United States, 28.3 percent had experienced childhood physical abuse.[4]

How Many Times?

A middle-aged woman came into my counseling office and said she was finally ready to deal with what happened to her as a child. Shortly before turning ten years old, she had been raped by a neighbor. The man was arrested, and her family had been loving and supportive. Yet as she shared, it was apparent that the single event had stretched its tentacles of blame, shame, and self-hatred around every aspect of her life and life decisions. Every time a good job, boyfriend, or opportunity arose, she either sabotaged it or chose an option that was not as good. Deep inside, that's what she felt she deserved—the not so good.

Some have shared that the beatings they received occurred whenever their father's favorite sports team lost. Others have said it was only a few times a year, when that particular extended-family member came to visit, while some have shared of daily abuse. One woman stated that her father would rape her the same night each week—the night her mother was gone to a weekly meeting. Others I've counseled have recounted tales of nightly abuse that lasted for years.

Whether you experienced abuse one time or a thousand times, it is all abuse. It is a violation. It is trauma.

It is wrong. Maybe you experienced abuse once, while others experienced it on a daily, weekly, or monthly basis for years. Some experienced a brutal rape; others, fondling; some, sodomy; and others experienced beatings and broken bones. Abuse is abuse, no matter how many times, what type, or how long.

> In every case of abuse, the dignity and beauty of the soul have been violated. Therefore, damage will be present whether one has been struck by a Mack truck travelling fifty miles per hour, or "merely" hit by a tricycle rolling at the same speed.[5]

Abuse is abuse, no matter how many times, what type, or how long.

Revictimization

In my first support group for female adolescent victims of sexual abuse (twenty-five years ago), the girls would share: "I was abused by my stepdad when I was eight years old," or "I was six when my uncle started." Others would add, "It was my cousin when I was twelve years old," or "The abuser began coming into my room at night when I was seven."

But now, things have changed—for the worse. A few years ago, I again led a sexual-abuse support group for adolescent girls. Here's what the girls would share:

*The first time, it was my dad, and I was six years old;
then my neighbor when I was nine.*

*It was only my stepdad in the beginning, and then my
older stepbrothers joined in.*

*I was five the first time, and it was my teacher. Then
it was my grandmother when I was eight, and my
aunt when I was eleven.*

Do you see the difference? Many victims have been victimized by more than one person. They have experienced multiple abuse situations by multiple people.

One woman I counseled shared that she'd been sexually abused by her grandfather, uncle, and father. After that, she was physically and sexually abused by an older brother. To top it off, her mother began to verbally and emotionally abuse her, blaming her and calling her a slut.

Did you know that, once abused, you are more susceptible to being used, abused, assaulted, coerced, and/or exploited again? Research overwhelmingly confirms that victims of trauma and abuse are much more likely to be revictimized.[6] This confirms the importance of joining this journey toward healing. Those who don't are more likely to become a victim again.

Whether frequent or infrequent, occurring over a short period of time or lasting years, abuse is wrong and it is traumatic.

My Experience

When I was _____ years old, I was abused for the first time.

I was abused again at age _____.

It happened again when I was _____ and _____ years old.

It happened: ___once ___# times ___daily ___ weekly ___about every month.

Most often, it happened (time of day, certain day of week, etc.) _____

The abuse went on for ____#

___years ___months ___weeks ___days.

Reflections

Thoughts, feelings, drawings, notes, or doodles

CHAPTER 6

Who Abuses?

A teenage girl I counseled had been abused by her mother's boyfriend. A leader in the community who knew about the situation, and who had a teenage daughter, offered to let her live with his family. Not much time passed, and he began sexually abusing the teen as well. When she finally told what was happening, the community turned on her. She was called a liar, and the community backed the leader, describing him as "an upright citizen who wouldn't do such a thing." Fortunately, it went to trial, and the courts found the community leader guilty.

Offenders are often viewed by outsiders as caring adults or devoted parents. Behind closed doors, a different story exists. Children are beaten beyond corrective discipline, chastised by dunking their hands in hot water, left alone in closets for long periods of time, and/or forced to perform sexual acts.

Anyone can be an abuser—whether devoted father, upright citizen, caring caregiver, or wealthy woman—yes, anyone.

Similar to the abused, abusers come from all races and religions, ages, wages, stages, genders, and generations. Both males and females are abused, and both males and females abuse.

Perhaps you've heard it said, "All abusers were abused, but not all who are abused become abusers." Just because you were abused doesn't mean you will become an abuser. That said, however, those who do become abusers were themselves abused. One study reported that nearly 30 percent of those who experienced childhood abuse or neglect "will later abuse their own children, thus continuing the horrible cycle of abuse."[7] This finding stresses the importance of addressing our own past abuse. Facing past abuse with courage and determination aids in our journey to break this atrocious cycle.

Facing your abuse and dealing with the negative emotional and behavioral side effects is a definite way to destroy the possibility of the abused becoming abusers.

Relationships

Not only are both males and females the abusers, their victims are also both male and female. Whichever type of abuse, it is not uncommon for a male or female to victimize someone of the same gender. This is especially true with physical and emotional abuse and neglect. That is, not all physical abuse is conducted by a father figure. I once had the honor of counseling a man who, as a child, suffered horrendous physical and emotional abuse at the hands of his mother.

With sexual abuse, it is generally more common that the abuser is someone of the opposite sex—but not always. One of the first books I read on child abuse had quite an impact on my growing awareness. It included chapters on father-son incest, mother-daughter incest, and sibling incest.[8] I've journeyed with women who, as girls, were abused by a female teacher, cousin, mentor, and aunt. I know of little boys being abused by a coach, a big brother, uncle, and priest. Not all sexual abuse is perpetrated on a victim of the opposite gender.

Facts

The majority of those who hurt and abuse minors are known to the victim. In fact, most are family members or those living inside the home. According to one report, 90.3 percent of the perpetrators of child abuse are family. That is, more than 80 percent were a parent, 6.1 percent were other relatives, and 4.2 percent were unmarried partners of parents.[9]

A small percentage of the sexually abused are violated by an unknown person. Hence, the former advisory to beware of "stranger danger" is misleading.

When referring to sexual abuse, offenders are overwhelmingly male, ranging from adolescents to the elderly. Some perpetrators are female. It is estimated that women are the abusers in about 14 percent of cases reported among boys and 6 percent of cases reported among girls. Approximately one-third of offenders are themselves juveniles, with 23 percent of reported cases of child sexual abuse perpetrated by individuals under the age of eighteen.[10]

Perpetrators of physical abuse are also primarily family members, those related to, and/or living in the home, of the victim. And as already stated, abusers often violate victims in more than one way. One person in counseling was physically, sexually, emotionally, and spiritually abused by family members.

Silent Partner

Silent partner is a term used to describe a non-offending caregiver who either knew about or suspected the abuse, but did nothing to stop it. In one story, a mother admitted that she had allowed her boyfriend access to her daughter because she was afraid if she didn't, he would leave her.

I've heard such comments as the following:

> *My mom knew it was happening because she'd hear me and dad fighting, then see the bruises and black eyes later. She never said or did anything.*
>
> *My dad came into the room when my grandfather was touching me, but turned around and walked out.*
>
> *I think my older sister knew about what was going on with her boyfriend and me.*
>
> *Our neighbors knew; they had to have known—but didn't do anything.*
>
> *When my mom was sick, she'd encouraged me to spend more time with my stepdad. I think I knew why.*

Dysfunctional Family Traits

Though not all abuse occurs within the family, we now know that the majority of abuse does. What are some of the characteristics of an abusive family—whether physical, sexual, or emotional abuse or neglect?

- Lack of personal responsibility — blame and shame of family members
- Misuse of power, authority, and control
- Lack of, or poor, communication
- Enmeshed, blurred boundaries or codependency
- Lack of warmth, affirmation, affection, empathy
- Lack of forgiveness
- Social isolation
- Lack of trust, critical, judgmental
- Lack of respect for individuality or privacy
- Continual relationship problems
- Inconsistency (in discipline, affection, responses, relationships, etc.)

Grooming

With sexual abuse, perpetrators often groom, or gradually prepare, their victims. What starts as innocent, friendly, caring behavior eventually becomes secretive, intrusive, and inappropriate.

Offenders might incorporate some of the following (the words minor, child, and youth are used interchangeably):

- Seeks time alone with minor.
- Makes child feel special and different.
- Begins with "innocent" touch that would be considered appropriate (but none the less breaks the physical touch barrier).
- Gradually and "accidentally" begins touching private parts, whether in passing or while assisting a minor with bathing or putting on clothes or sunscreen.
- Doesn't respect privacy, whether in the bathroom or bedroom, often walking in when changing or undressed.
- Eventually introduces topics that include sexual content, indirectly at first. Later, the conversations may be directly about sex, sex education, body parts, arousal, sexual feelings, activities, and obligations. Also, words change from pretty or cute, to sexy, arousing, or sensual.
- Showing or asking to see private parts as a part of the child's needed sex education. Or intentionally allowing the perpetrator's naked body to be seen.
- Begins to share personal things about the perpetrator's sex life—involvements and desires—or those of others (such as parents, siblings, relatives, or teachers).
- Tells you not to tell or implies it because you'll get into trouble; no one will believe you; he or she loves you; "it's our secret;" or many other statements, whether stated or implied.

Comply or Consent?

Those who abuse want you to think that you deserved, agreed with, or consented to the abuse. Some believe this themselves. They want to convince you that you are more responsible or to blame for what happened than you actually are. The message is that you complied and you consented—which is absolutely absurd. Even if you enjoyed the attention or the bodily sensations of sexual abuse, or wanted the anger release or punishment to deaden the pain of physical abuse, or welcomed the self-affirming negative rants of verbal abuse—you did not initially agree to abuse.

If you were physically and verbally abused, you probably thought it was due to some disobedience or fault of your own. Besides, you probably didn't even know that the behavior was abusive. Therefore, you bit the bullet, got tougher, tried harder, avoided more, and kept quiet. Did you comply? Yes. Did you consent? No.

When we disobey as children, we may need discipline and guidance but we never deserve physical abuse. No disobedience gives a parent or someone in authority permission to abuse us. Punishment is punitive and should be replaced by positive parenting and corrective discipline. Child rearing should never be abusive.

You may have thought that you agreed to or consented to the abuse because of your silence (addressed later in this book).

As already stated, many who are sexually abused are confused and unaware that what happened was wrong and illegal. When a thirteen-year-old girl is forced to do sexual things with a much-older boy, that is abuse. When a teacher has sex with a minor under his or her authority, even if the victim is a teenager, that is abuse. When there is an age difference and/or a position of authority over the minor, it is considered sexual abuse. Few, if any, exceptions apply. Even if you allowed the abuse, it is still abuse, whether you complied or thought you consented.

One victim shared that her older sister's boyfriend would force her to do sexual things with him. She stated, "Even though I didn't want it or like it, I didn't know it was against the law. I thought I had consented because I didn't tell anyone." Was she coerced? Yes. Did she comply? Yes. Did she consent? No.

My Experience

1. On the list below, indicate both the type of abuse and the relationship you have or had with your abuser(s). Place a P next to those who physically abused you, an S for sexual abuse, VE for verbal-emotional abuse, and N for neglect. You might have more than one letter by several of the relationships: P, S, VE, N.

Relationships

The people who abused you may have had this relationship with you. If not listed, write the relationship under "other."

___father   ___mother
___brother   ___sister
___uncle   ___aunt
___grandfather   ___grandmother
___cousin (male)   ___cousin (female)
___stepdad   ___stepmom
___stepbrother   ___stepsister
___mother's boyfriend   ___father's girlfriend
___sibling's friend   ___half-brother or sister
___youth leader   ___doctor/nurse/dentist
___coach   ___friend
___teacher/tutor   ___school staff or janitor
___boyfriend   ___girlfriend
___friend's parent   ___parent's friend
___priest/pastor/rabbi   ___stranger(s)
___store/business worker   ___coworker
___neighbor   ___mentor
___Other: _____

Some survivors experience abuse from one perpetrator, and others have suffered different types of abuse from one or numerous people. Most offenders have many victims.

2. When you are done, complete the following section. Write your age; the type(s) of abuse; the relationship of the abuser(s) to you; and, if you're ready and willing, their names as well.

When I was _____ years old I was (*type of abuses*) _____abused by (*name*) _____, my (*relationship*) _____.
I was abused again at age _____. It was _____ abuse by _____, my _____, and at _____ years old, I was _____ abused by _____, my_____.

3. If you wrote the person's name, how did you feel (glad, regretful, sad, numb, vengeful, angry, good)?

4. Who else was in the area (house, building, etc.) when you were being abused (*parents, siblings, neighbors, other teachers, etc.*)?

_____.
I think (name) _____ knew that something was going on.

I know (name) _____ saw something going on and knew about the abuse.

I think the perpetrator may have also molested
_____ and _____.

5. Comply and consent

___ I complied with the abuse and felt I deserved it.
___ I complied with what was happening to me but didn't like it and thought I didn't deserve it.
___ I was coerced or forced to do things I didn't want to do. I didn't think I had a choice.
___ I thought that I consented because I said nothing and told no one.
___ I now know that I didn't really consent.

Reflections

Thoughts, feelings, drawings, notes, and doodles

CHAPTER 7

Where Abuse Happens

Most victims are abused in houses or buildings. Some are abused in cars or other vehicles. Therefore, I wasn't quite prepared for one story I was told, feeling a bit stunned on the inside, and trying not to let it show on the outside. Nancy had been abused in a culvert—*a culvert*. That's a large drainage pipe used as a water duct or for sewage. *For sewage!* That's probably how she felt: dirty, smelly, unwanted, get-it-out, and get-it-away sewage.

Another person shared that her numerous abuse episodes happened in a barn, with the squealing of pigs and the putrid smell of manure accosting her nostrils. She shared of feeling treated like she was just another animal to control, tame, and dominate.

Abuse can happen anywhere, anytime.

Where

Abuse can happen in the bedroom, bathroom, or kitchen; in public or in private; on foreign soil or at home.

Abuse can be well planned or spontaneous; anticipated or shockingly unpredicted. It can happen anywhere at anytime.

I've heard or read of incidences of abuse happening in boats, at street fairs, in a synagogue, at a dentist's office, on the playground, in a basement, on a workbench, and so on. One survivor I met was gang raped at an amusement park while on vacation with her family in another country.

> *I begged my mom to get a lock put on the bathroom door because he would come in while I was showering.*
> *When he'd get really, really mad, he'd drag me down to the basement to "teach me a lesson".*
> *He took me into the storage closet at school.*
> *I can still picture the board in the barn that he'd use to beat me.*

Home

The vast majority of abuse—whether physical, sexual, emotional, or neglect—happens in one's own home, the place that is supposed to be safe, warm, and loving. How was *home* for you?

When you think about your home growing up, are your memories more positive or negative?

Did you feel safe?

Where did you most feel safe? Unsafe?

Where did you go when you were angry, alone, or sad?

Locations

Here's a list of some of the places where victims have been abused:

____In my home

____At a friend's house

____At a relative's house

____At a neighbor's house

____In the living room

____In the family room

____In the bedroom

____In the bathroom

____In the attic

____In the basement

____In the office, study

____In the kitchen, pantry

____At a park, playground

____In a barn, storage shed

____At a gym, sports field

____At a store, business, work

____At a carnival, party

____In a car, bus, vehicle

____On a boat, train, plane

____At school

____At a park or in the woods

____In a pool or hot tub

____In a tent

____In another country

____Mosque, church, synagogue (religious building)

____Underground (in a shelter, culvert, cave)

____In a public building (library, office, etc.)

____At doctor's or dentist's office

____In a dressing room, public bathroom

____In a tree house, kids' fort, playhouse

____Other: _____

Unfortunately, abuse can happen anywhere.

My Experience

Where. Complete the checklist above for all locations that applied to the abuse you experienced, adding any other locations that may not be listed.

Most often I was abused in/at (location)

_____, _____

and in/at _____.

____ I get triggered with bad memories when I'm back in that place again.

____ I get triggered with bad memories when I'm in places similar to where I was primarily abused.

____ I can go there now and not feel too anxious, angry, sad, or self-condemning.

____ I still avoid the place or places like where I was abused.

____ I feel _____ when I'm back in that place or in a similar type of place.

Reflections

Thoughts, feelings, drawings, notes, or doodles

The Reactions, Responses, Thoughts, and Feelings

*"Anyone can hide. Facing up to
things, working through them,
that's what makes you strong."*
— SARAH DESSEN

CHAPTER 8

How Our Bodies React

Our bodies sometimes react without our permission. Something happens and the next thing we know, our bodies have taken control, and we don't have a say in the matter. This is what happens during a trauma.

Fight, Flee, Freeze

When we are threatened, our response is to fight, flee, or freeze. This is part of our innate defense system. When we are unable to engage the fight or flight responses, we instinctively utilize the freezing response. It is not a conscious, voluntary choice, but an involuntary physiological response. That is, we don't choose it, it happens whether we want it or not.

> "Physiologists call this... the ''immobility' or 'freezing' response. It is one of the three primary responses available... when faced with an

overwhelming threat. A traumatized person's nervous system is not damaged, it is frozen in a kind of suspended animation."[11]

Over the years, I have spoken with many who have felt deep shame and guilt for not having fought back or fled the abusive situation. Both of these options seem to bring less shame than freezing. "If only I'd yelled or screamed or kicked or…" And yet so many realize that, at the time, it was not really an option. Or later say, "I should have run away and gotten out of there." Again, it feels like a retrospective, critical, improbable assessment. You are so hard on yourselves for doing something over which you had no control.

Freezing indicates involuntary compliance. Even if you seemed to *allow* the abuse to happen, this reaction is often the result of your internal, generally subconscious, assessment that it would be dangerous to resist. This seeming compliance can be due to the desire to avoid punishment, to fit in, or to not cause problems. Going along with the abuse may also be due to thinking that what was happening was normal or okay. (This is discussed more in coming chapters.)

Don't be so hard on yourself. Remember that you were assessing the situation with your child's brain that was not yet fully developed.

With freezing, however, the body assesses the danger and makes the decision for us. It is normal and common for abuse victims to freeze (not fight or flee) during the trauma (abuse).

In *Waking the Tiger—Healing Trauma* (1997), author Levine summarizes it well:

> "When neither fight or flight will ensure safety, there is another line of defense: immobility (freezing) which is just as universal and basic to survival. This defense strategy is rarely given equal billing in texts... yet freezing... is an equally viable survival strategy in threatening situations. In many situations, it is the best choice... It is not a sign of inadequacy or weakness."[12]

Whether we froze or didn't run or fight, too many victims carry extra shame and blame for not responding more forcefully to the abuser.

> *When I learned that what I did (freeze) was what many, if not most, victims do, I was relieved. For years, I'd felt so ashamed for not doing anything when I was being abused.*

My Experience

When the abuse/trauma happened, my reaction was to:
___Fight ___Flee ___Freeze
___Comply *(thinking there was no other option)*

(Check those that apply)

___ I have carried much guilt and shame from believing that I didn't respond right.

___ I still believe I could or should have responded differently.

___ I wish I fought back (screamed louder, kicked harder, etc.).

___ At first, I felt ashamed because I froze, but now I know that it wasn't wrong. It was a normal response.

___ I complied because I felt I had no choice.

___ I complied because I was scared.

___ I complied because I thought it was "normal" or okay.

___ Other: _____

___ Other: _____

Reflections

Thoughts, feelings, drawings, notes, or doodles

CHAPTER 9

How Our Minds React

t's human nature to try to rationalize, minimize, or justify a situation. We're good at it. Every time I pass a police car, I begin this process and plan what I will say if pulled over. When unexpected or unwanted situations arise, our human nature kicks in and we label, categorize, fit in a box, and try to understand what is going on. Sometimes we get it right, sometimes we don't.

As you look at your reactions or initial thoughts after abuse, it's not fair to be the Monday quarterback, taking that after-the-fact perspective and analysis. You're looking at your thoughts and reactions, not your long-considered reflections. Your reactions are your attempt to make sense of what has happened, to categorize it, excuse it, and deal with it. These reactions are often unhelpful and get in the way of your healing process.

Possible Reactions

Here are some examples of what you may have thought:

- I *minimized* the abuse. I told myself, "It wasn't that bad." "It was only a few times." "It wasn't full intercourse."
- I *rationalized* the abuse. I told myself, "My dad was lonely." "My mom was stressed out." "We were poor."
- I tended to *deny* that the abuse really happened. I told myself, "You made it up." "It didn't really happen, I just imagined it." "You remember it wrong."
- I *blocked* the abuse from my memory. (Forgot that it happened or dissociated.)
- I told someone about the abuse, but then took it back (*recanted*), saying, "I made it up" because I didn't like what was happening.
- I *mislabeled* the abuse, thinking it was "just strict discipline," or "just being overly affectionate."

The extent of the trauma you experienced depends upon several factors. The younger you were, the longer and the more intrusive the abuse, the closeness of the offender, the absence of emotional support, and more, all contribute to the intensity of your trauma experience. Whether abuse happens one time or hundreds of times, whether it is physical abuse or sexual abuse, whether it happens at age six or sixteen, by a parent or a stranger, it is all trauma, and it is all a violation of the dignity and worth of the individual. Generally, however, the more traumas that are experienced, the more challenging the recovery process.

Some of the factors that affect the degree of trauma experienced are as follows:

- The age of the victim
- The age of the abuser(s)
- The relationship of the abuser(s) (relative versus stranger)
- The frequency of the abuse
- The type and number of different traumas (multiplicity of trauma events)
- The number of different perpetrators
- The length of the victimization (day, month, years)
- The extent of the trauma (intensity)
- Whether violence and threats were used (to self or others)
- Whether victim keeps silent or tells
- Whether victim, if tells, is helped or ignored
- Caregiver reaction if told (believing or blaming)
- Whether or not the victim has a loving, supportive caregiver/parent/environment
- The victim's personality and resiliency

(Becca C. Johnson, PhD, 1998)

My Experience

My Reactions to the Abuse

When the abuse happened, perhaps you told yourself: *(check all that apply)*

___I just thought it was strict discipline, not abuse.

___I didn't know it was wrong.

___I thought it was wrong, but wasn't sure.

___I knew it was wrong.

___I didn't think it was *that* bad.

___I enjoyed the attention.

___I enjoyed the way my body felt.

___I hated myself so much that I felt I deserved the harsh punishment (abuse).

___I thought it was normal or what families do.

___I wanted it to stop, but didn't know how.

___I didn't know what to do or who to talk to.

___I didn't want to tell anyone.

___I thought I was supposed to do it or put up with it.

___I thought it didn't matter.

___I didn't think I had any choice.

___ Other: _____

___ I realize that I've done the following with my abuse (check as many as apply):

___ rationalized ___denied ___blocked ___mislabeled ___excused

___ I don't think the way I've labeled what happened is healthy or good for me.

___ I still believe most of what I checked.

___ I used to have some of these thoughts, but now I know that what happened really was wrong.

Reflections

Thoughts, feelings, drawings, notes, or doodles

CHAPTER 10

What We Were Told

Have you ever heard someone say, "Don't believe everything you're told?" But then you were probably also told, "Listen to your elders and do what they say." These certainly are confusing and conflicting messages. When you were a minor, you actually didn't have the brain ability to question or analyze. Your brain was busy soaking in knowledge and learning, but wasn't fully developed and able to evaluate or discern what was going on around you. So, if an adult told you something, you generally believed it.

Those who abuse use various statements to coerce, force, shame, blame, demand, and degrade their victims into compliance. Sometimes these are said aloud, sometimes they are not. They want you to believe what they are saying or not saying (but clearly inferred). They have a strategy and use tactics to get you to keep quiet. The statements or beliefs that you may have been told, whether directly stated or unspoken, can be summarized in this list of commonly used offender tactics:

___Blame and shame the victim
___Imply mutual consent and/or enjoyment
___Imply victim blame and responsibility
___Make verbal, physical, and/or emotional threats
___Imply or say that nothing is wrong with the sexual acts
___Imply or say that no one cares
___Imply or say that no one will believe the victim
___Imply or say that the victim is worthless and deserves such treatment
___Make promises of future benefits—bribery or incentives (of gifts, events, care, etc.)
___Make promises of future behavior (not to harm sibling or others if victim complies)
___Use force, fraud, or coercion
___Threaten harm and/or the loss of basic needs
___Deceive and tell lies
___Other: _____
___Other: _____

Whether said aloud or not, the communication was generally loud and clear, and clearly understood. The following statements represent those that you may have heard, whether spoken or *implied*. Some of these refer to one or multiple types of abuse (whether neglect or sexual, physical, and/or emotional abuse).

Spoken or implied statements by abusers include the following:

___ It's because you're so pretty that I do these things.

___ I will hurt you if you tell anyone.

___ Let this be our little secret.

___ I will hurt (or kill) your pet if you tell anyone.

___ This is fun, isn't it?

___ You must apologize for making me feel this way (i.e., angry, sexually stimulated)

___ Nothing was said, but it was clearly understood not to say anything.

___ I will hurt your _____ (mom, dad, family) if you tell or if you don't obey.

___ I will abuse your sister or brother if you don't do what I say.

___ I do this because I love you (to show my love)

___ This is because you are a bad little girl (boy).

___ This is your punishment.

___ Sex is a beautiful thing.

___ I am supposed to teach you these things (i.e., sexual acts).

___ You are worthless (a whore, slut, filthy, stupid, dirty).

___ You deserve this (being used, abused, hit, beat, yelled at).

___ I will teach you to enjoy this.

___ The way *you* dressed made me do this.

___ You're a dirty (naughty) girl or boy.

___ I am your father (and you are supposed to obey me).

___ There's nothing wrong with what we do.

___ I'm glad you like it too.

___ It's *your* fault.

___ If you do this, I won't _____.

___ If you do this, you will (be popular, liked, accepted, desirable, sexy; or get that toy, clothes, electronics that you want).

___ Don't tell, or it'll be on Facebook or YouTube.

___ If you do this, I'll help you (go to college, get a job, become famous, etc.).

___ You won't get any food (clothes, bed, love), unless you do what I say.

___ You are promiscuous.

___ God made sex. He wants us to do this.

___ Your parents know about this and say it is okay.

___ Other: _____

My Experience

1. Return to the first list in this chapter and place a check next to those tactics used on you that are commonly employed by offenders. Add any other tactics you may have experienced.

2. Return to this last list and place a check next to the statements you heard or that were implied. Also, add any other statements you may have heard. Put an X if you believed it then; if you still believe it, circle the X.

3. How was it for you to think about what was directly or indirectly communicated to you about the abuse?

Reflections

Thoughts, feelings, drawings, notes, or doodles

CHAPTER 11

Why We Keep Silent

Years ago, I co-led a support group for mothers of children who had been abused. Can you guess what question was most asked by the moms? It wasn't, "How could this have happened?" or "Why *my* child?" or "Why didn't I see it?" or even "Why!?" The most asked question was, "Why didn't my child tell me?"

A teenager was raped at a party. A friend who found out about it recommended she not tell anyone. "No one will believe you. Everyone will think it's your fault. You'll get blamed. Everyone will act weird around you if it gets out." The girl, like most victims, kept quiet and let the pain and shame brew inside like a poisonous potion. Fortunately for her, it didn't ferment for as long as most. When she spoke up and spit out what had happened, hope and healing began.

Maybe you, like most victims, didn't speak out during the abuse, but now is the time. Get it out and get going on your healing journey. Don't beat yourself up for not having spoken sooner. The cards were stacked against you—against most victims. Disclosing the abuse, telling others, and reporting what happened is a monumental and seemingly unsurmountable task. Read on, and you'll understand why. Hopefully you'll be more grace giving to yourself.

There are many reasons why victims of abuse and exploitation do not speak out. It is hard for others to understand. The shaming power of abuse, the fear of possible repercussions, and negative responses from others all contribute to why victims remain silent.

Why you kept silent is more easily understood after reading the chapters on *What We Feel* and *What We Think*. When you feel ashamed, responsible, distrusting, trapped, threatened, scared, overwhelmed, helpless, and/or hopeless, the likelihood you will disclose the abuse is low.

Silence Compliance Model
(Becca C. Johnson, PhD, 2011)

To help understand the silencing power of abuse, I developed what I call The Silence Compliance Model.[13] It categorizes the many reasons why victims don't tell what is happening or happened. Some of the reasons overlap, but this model illustrates several of the key factors contributing to why many trauma victims remain silent. The three categories are coercion, collusion, and contrition, or scared, survival, and shame.

Coercion involves the use of force or threats to make someone do something against his or her will. Synonyms include force, cruelty, intimidation, oppression, and compulsion. The victim is *scared* and remains silent due to fear of cruelty, brutality, threats of deprivation, and/ or threats to one's safety or the safety of others.

Collusion involves the seeming cooperation or compliance. In the case of a victim-perpetrator relationship, this is actually due to force, fraud, deception, and/or control. It may seem that the victim is voluntarily cooperating, but this happens because he or she believes that consent and involvement are mandatory. The victim does whatever is necessary to *survive*. He or she may experience helplessness, a dependence upon and/or love toward the offender, or even brainwashing (a distorted or limited view of reality due to isolation). The threats may also be accompanied by occasional kindnesses. This is also called Stockholm Syndrome, but I refer to this as *captive compliance.*

Contrition conveys the overwhelming and deep feelings of *shame*, guilt, and remorse experienced by the traumatized. Victims feel contrite when they believe they are responsible for the abuse. They mistakenly believe they had control over the abuse, blaming themselves for not having tried harder, known better, or for having trusted. Blame and shame, feelings of worthlessness and hopelessness, along with fear of rejection, abandonment, and stigmatization, keep them silent.

Some Interesting Facts

Did you know the following regarding cases of sexual abuse?

- Fewer than one in four sexual abuse survivors disclose immediately after the abuse occurs.

- A majority of victims keep it to themselves, never disclosing what happened. When or if they do tell, it is generally many years later (typically eight to fifteen years). Most who experience child sexual assault do not disclose until adulthood, and many never tell at all.[14]
- Some victims tell and then recant (take back) the disclosure of abuse, due to the repercussions or consequences experienced.
- Nondisclosure, delayed disclosure, and recanting (retraction) are much more likely in cases in which the perpetrator is close to the victim.[15] Victims of physical abuse are much less likely to break the silence about their abuse because most do not identify it as abuse or believe the abuser's blaming of them—that they caused or deserved it. Many family interactions contribute to abuse when using the silent treatment (withholding affection and interaction when a family member has been disobedient or not done what's expected) or walking on eggshells (fear that someone will blow up and get angry). These unpredictable and uncertain communication responses can lead to insecurity and a reluctance to share. Other families have communication styles that include spoken or unspoken messages that could be described as controlling, in denial, enmeshed (poor boundaries), blaming and shaming, confused, appeasing, or volatile. These unhealthy communication patterns make it hard for victims to speak up and out about the abuse.

Reasons for Not Disclosing the Abuse

A study of victim silence grouped the reasons as follows:[16]

- **Threats made by the perpetrator**
  Threats of violence, getting in trouble, having no friends or money, or parents' anger.
- **Fears**
  Fear of the perpetrator; negative repercussions and emotions by caregivers; what would or could happen to the victim; possible consequences of telling; being judged; or being forced to leave home.
- **Lack of opportunity**
  Not knowing who or how to tell or having the opportunity to tell.
- **Lack of understanding**
  Not understanding what is or isn't abuse; what would happen if they told; and not wanting others to know.
- **Relationship with the perpetrator**
  The victim expressing positive emotions toward perpetrator, relative, or friend, or wanting to maintain the relationship even amid the abuse.

Disbelieving and blaming the victim can compound the damage done by the trauma. We must continue to discover ways of making the unspeakable safely speakable, and thus promote healing.[17]

My Experience

Complete the following by checking as many as apply to your situation(s).

When the abuse(s) happened, I told (disclosed)
___right away ___much later ___never
___someone else told ___now is the first time

I kept silent (didn't tell anyone) because:
___I was too young and didn't have the words or under-standing to tell anyone.
___I didn't know it was wrong, so I didn't tell anyone.
___I was afraid for my safety.
___I was afraid for my family's safety.
___I was afraid of what my family would think.
___I was afraid of what others would think.
___I was afraid others would blame me.
___I was afraid of what might happen.
___I was afraid of what would happen to the abuser.
___I was afraid the abuser would stop loving me.
___I was afraid people would think I'm a bad person.
___I was afraid no one would believe me.
___I was afraid for my younger siblings.
___I was afraid I'd get in trouble.
___I was afraid my parent would get mad.
___I felt helpless and hopeless.
___I feared being abandoned and rejected.
___I was ashamed.
___I didn't know I could or should tell.
___I thought it was my fault.
___I enjoyed the attention and didn't want it to stop.

___I enjoyed the physical touch (stimulation) and didn't want the abuse to stop.

___I thought I'd get in trouble.

___I pretended that it didn't happen.

___I was afraid our family would fall apart if I told.

___I didn't know who to tell.

___I didn't know who I could trust.

___I didn't want to stop getting what I received (candy, toys, money, clothes, etc.).

___I was dependent on abuser (financially, emotionally).

___ Other: _____

___ Other: _____

Reflections

Thoughts, feelings, drawings, notes, or doodles

CHAPTER 12

How We Feel

asked, "What do you feel when you think about what happened to you as a child?"

> *Numb, most of the time I just feel numb. Then, at other times, I feel intense rage, so intense that I worry what I might do.* He paused and then continued. *If I'm not feeling those, I'm usually drowning in anxiety, depression, or self-hatred.*

Shame, blame, rejection, fear, guilt, hopelessness, helplessness, anger, anxiety, betrayal, confusion, and grief are but a few of the many emotions you may experience. Each of these alone can be crushing, but when you experience a combination of these simultaneously, it can be overpowering and devastating.

Victims feel overwhelming powerlessness, scary fear, and depressing grief.

Unwanted, engulfing, and constant emotions flood the hearts of those who have been abused. That's why so many act out, become angry or depressed, or shut down their feelings. When it's too painful to feel, many attempt to numb the emotions with denial, food, or substances.

> I was <u>sad</u> all the time but didn't really know why. I was too young to understand.
>
> The <u>panic attacks</u> would come at random times. I couldn't control them. I hated it!
>
> I got to the point where I felt that everything was my fault. (<u>guilt</u>)
>
> The <u>anger</u> consumed me and controlled me. I was mad at everything and everyone.
>
> I was <u>afraid</u> for my sister, my family—what others would think and of anyone finding out.
>
> I <u>blamed</u> myself for everything that happened. I was filled with <u>shame</u>.
>
> I became so <u>anxious</u> and controlling. I was horrible to live with.

Common Victim Feelings

Fear

You may have experienced fear of bodily harm, fear of the loss of the affection received from the abuser, fear of the possibility of a broken home, fear of the future, fear for your lives, fear of loneliness, fear of the abuse being disclosed, or fear of the abuse not being disclosed. While safety and fear of physical harm are common, the majority of fears focus on emotional and relational concerns.

> *I was more afraid of what others thought of me than of the abuse.*
> *Fear of being hurt, fear of others finding out, fear of rejection. I had a lot of fears.*

Anger and Disgust

You may have experienced anger or disgust at the offender, at the non-offending parent(s), at yourself, at God (or karma or fate), and at others. While anger at the offender is considered appropriate, you may feel more anger at yourself than at the perpetrator. Much of your anger may also be directed at the (generally unknowing) non-offending parent(s) who didn't provide adequate protection or help in the healing process. Or you may be angry at those who, in an attempt to help, actually revictimize you by their insensitive remarks or expectations. Many, if not most, victims feel disgust toward themselves for not having done something to stop what was happening.

> *I remember hating myself and wishing he would hurt me so bad that I'd die.*
> *The anger was eating me up inside because I kept it there and didn't let it out.*
> *I was so disgusted with everything and everyone, especially myself.*

Guilt

You may have taken responsibility for what happened, blaming yourself. Whether directly told that you were to blame or self-imposed, you incorrectly believe you are at fault for the abuse. Thus, guilt floods the heart.

I always believed it was my fault.
I think guilt has been the root belief that led to many of my problems.

Shame

Shame has been defined as humiliating disgrace. It implies that I am not only to blame for doing something wrong, but what I did is disgusting and offensive. "Because I did a bad thing, I am a bad person." Guilt leads to shame. We can feel guilty (responsible) about something without feeling ashamed (I'm a bad person). Unfortunately, most of the abused not only feel guilty about the abuse, they also feel that they are worthless, shameful, and despicable.

I felt completely worthless, a nobody.
Guilt and shame have been my companions for many, many years.

Depression and Loneliness

Profound sadness, inner angst, fatigue, loss of energy, lack of enjoyment, apathy, difficulty concentrating, eating and sleep problems, hopelessness, low self-esteem (feelings of worthlessness), and suicidal thoughts are all common symptoms of depression. It has been referred to as anger turned inward, and plagues most abuse victims.

> *I cried a lot when I was little, but most of the time it was when I was alone.*
>
> *Being in bed alone at night was the hardest for me. The sadness and loneliness overwhelmed me. I felt that no one cared or understood me or what was going on.*
>
> *I think my depression was rooted in my low self-esteem. I felt like a nobody.*

Confused, Overwhelmed, and Hyperalert

Feeling confused and/or overwhelmed is all too common among abuse victims. Uncertainty, doubts, questions, suspicions, and mistrust go hand in hand with caution, fear, hypervigilance, and a feeling of impending abuse. Questioning yourself and how to label what's happening, you are left confused and overwhelmed. The unpredictability of most abuse leaves you on red-alert, wasting energy that should be spent on schoolwork or other activities and pursuits.

> *I felt like I was always on high alert, waiting for something to happen.*
>
> *It was like I was living in a fog, unable to see clearly what was going on and always feeling stressed out and worried.*

Betrayal

Many abuse victims experience profound betrayal by their perpetrator, especially if they had a close relationship. Some refer to this as *betrayal trauma* because it deeply alters your worldview, beliefs about trust, relationships, love, kindness, safety, and more. Sex offenders, known to the minor initially, develop a loving connection, build trust, and display appropriate physical contact before beginning abusive behaviors. You feel betrayed, not only by the offender, but also by your own natural human longings for closeness, nurturance, and affection. Physical abuse, generally by a family member, betrays the role of being a *caregiver*.

> *I loved him and I trusted him—and he betrayed me. That hurts so deeply.*
> *I still want to think that all the abuse was a big mistake, that he really is good.*

Control and Hopelessness (Trapped)

You didn't get to choose or control when, where, how, how often, or with whom you would be abused. Like most people, you probably tried to control your circumstances. Children will try to get better grades, keep their room cleaner, wear different clothes, and keep their mouths shut, all in an effort to hopefully change the outcome—abuse. They will try over and over again, thinking they have the ability—whether by deed or behavior—to somehow change the abuser's actions. These attempts continually meet with failure until the victim realizes the sense of powerlessness. Once this happens, depression, despair, and hopelessness set in.

I tried and tried to do things to get it to stop, but it never did—until I left home.
I think I developed some OCD tendencies because of the abuse. I was always trying to control everything.
The harder I tried, the worse it got.

Ambivalence

Ambivalence occurs when you experience two oppositional feelings at the same time. You may have both loved *and* hated the abuser. You may love and hate the special or harmful attention you received. You may feel you deserved the punishment because "I'm a bad person," but at the same time, you may feel that you don't deserve it. You may hate the molestation, yet feel pleasurable arousal when abused. And you may both love and despise your longing for human contact and affection.

I loved him, and I hated him.
I felt like I was going crazy inside, trying to tell myself that this nice person wasn't really doing such horrible things to me.

Victim Reality: Common Feelings from an Uncommon Experience[18]

The following list of words beginning with the letter "*d*" was developed to help demonstrate the depth of emotional devastation experienced by those abused or exploited:

- distrusting
- doubt-filled
- dependent
- dissociative
- dreamless
- depressed
- discouraged
- devastated
- dejected
- damaged-goods
- disregarded
- demoralized
- down-trodden
- demeaned
- disposable
- dehumanized
- defiled
- devalued
- deceived
- dirty
- desperate
- disconnected
- destroyed
- detached
- dumb
- dead

My Experience

1. This list includes the most common emotions survivors feel. Put an X next to those feelings on the list below that you have experienced, but no longer feel. Circle those emotions you *still* feel when you think about what happened to you.

I felt/still feel _____ (emotions) about the abuse and what happened.

___Fearful   ___Special
___To blame   ___Loved
___Shame   ___Excited
___Deceived   ___Aroused
___Guilty   ___Dirty
___Angry   ___Stupid
___Sad   ___Anxious, worried
___Confused (ambivalent)   ___Numb
___Betrayed   ___Helpless
___Embarrassed   ___Hopeless or depressed
___Stuck   ___Powerless
___Sneaky   ___Other: _____

2. *Overwhelming feelings.* Check those statements below that you felt about yourself and your situation.

___I felt dirty.
___I felt stupid.
___I didn't want to do anything that I used to enjoy.
___I felt exhausted and lethargic.
___I worried a lot.

___I cried a lot.

___I wanted to scream a lot.

___I found it hard to think or focus.

___I hated myself.

___I hated my caregiver *(non-offending)*.

___I hated the person who hurt me.

___I felt I was a bad person.

___I was scared, afraid of what could happen.

___I was afraid I'd get in trouble.

___I felt lonely.

___I felt like nobody cared about me.

___I felt like I'd never be normal.

___I felt like I was to blame for everything.

___I didn't know who to trust or what to do.

___I felt ashamed about what happened.

___I was frustrated, discouraged, depressed.

___I felt confused or like it wasn't real.

___I yearned for the attention and interaction.

What have you learned about yourself and your feelings?

Reflections

Thoughts, feelings, drawings, notes, or doodles

CHAPTER 13

Where We Direct the Anger

Over and over again, as I've worked with survivors of abuse, it is apparent that their anger becomes misdirected. When asked about anger, the response is often one extreme or the other—reporting no anger or excessive preoccupation with anger. But it's not so much the amount of anger that concerns me, but rather where it is directed.

I ask the following, "When you feel angry about what happened, at whom is that anger directed: the offender, a parent(s), God, self, someone else? With whom are you most angry? Next angry? The least angry?" I am no longer surprised at the common response.

At whom do you think most survivors place the majority of their anger? At the abuser (where it *should* belong)? At an non-protective parent? At God?

Most survivors' greatest anger is directed at the person in the mirror—themselves.

If you were told, or it was implied, that the abuse was your fault and you believed it, chances are you too have focused your anger at the wrong person.

Self-blame and the continual belief that "I should have known better or tried harder" plague victims so much that their anger becomes misguided.

If you believe that what happened was your fault, then you are more likely to blame and direct most of the anger at yourself. You *must* break the blame cycle and shed the self-loathing and anger if you are to heal and move past victim to survivor.

As you acknowledge the true source of blame and responsibility for the abuse, you are free to feel anger toward your offender(s), and then release that anger so that it doesn't grow into bitterness.

My Experience

Place a number next to each person listed below, ranking where they fit on your anger scale.

1 = most of my anger ➜ 5 = the least amount of my anger is directed at that person.

The Focus of My Anger: When I'm angry about what happened, it is usually directed at... (1–5)

___Abuser

___Self

___Caregiver (parent)

___God

___ Other (police, foster parent, friend, and so on)
Write who: _____

___ Someone else? _____

Check all statements below that apply to you:

___ I still blame myself.

___ I tend to excuse the abuser more than I excuse myself.

___ I tend to direct my anger at myself.

___ I need to redirect my anger at the abuser.

___ I need to not be so hard on myself.

___ I need to forgive myself.

___ Other: _____

Reflections

Thoughts, feelings, drawings, notes, or doodles

CHAPTER 14

What We Think

Not long ago, I led a 10-week support group for sexually abused teenage girls. I decided that we would end each session with a group cheer, putting our hands together in the center and loudly shouting our slogan. Well, as you might imagine, the idea didn't go over well. With rolling eyes and slumped postures the girls' body language shouted, "This is stupid!" which was not the desired cheer. But I persisted amid the resistance and said, "Come on, let's do it." One by one, they hesitantly joined hands and sheepishly and softly said our new group cheer. I decided not to complain at the weakness of the exercise and thanked them for doing it.

As the weeks progressed, the session-ending cheer got louder and stronger. Our final session ended with a resounding, bold shout: "Don't believe the lies!"

Lies—that's what I call the many incorrect thoughts victims develop as a result of being abused. Whether you call it cognitive distortions, false thinking, distorted thought processes, or unwanted thoughts, it's all the same—unhelpful and unhealthy.

As you've already learned, most wrong thinking is related to your self-blame for what happened. Other unhelpful thoughts come from the distrust and betrayal you experienced, as well as your negative self-perceptions and newly formed assumptions about life and people (the now damaged worldview).

If we were to label or group your thought processes, they might include a sense of:

Negativity	*When things happen, they will be bad.*
Pervasiveness	*Everything is bad.*
Permanency	*Everything will always be bad.*
Personal responsibility	*Everything bad that happens is my fault.*

Dirty

After each incident of abuse, Chelsea took a shower. Even on days when she wasn't abused by her mom's boyfriend, she took multiple showers. She couldn't get clean enough. She often took three or four showers a day. It didn't help though. She still felt dirty on the inside.

The lies playing over and over again in her head judged her as "filthy, dirty, rotten, putrid, polluted, yuck!" The more these words bombarded her mind, the more she began to view them as absolute truth.

When I entered Chelsea's life, my singular voice was drowned by the multitude of thoughts, beliefs, and lies continually screaming in her head. One of the biggest battles in healing from abuse is in the mind. First, she had to be willing to hear what I was saying. Next, she had to take the big step to listen to what I was saying. Finally, she had to be willing to believe that what I shared could possibly be true. It took time. Eventually, Chelsea began to identify her long-held thoughts as lies and slowly grew to embrace the truth about her dignity and worth.

The Lies

After hearing so many of these harmful thoughts over the years, I decided to write down as many as I could remember. I gave the list to a group of adult women who had been sexually abused and exploited (prostituted). I asked these amazing survivors to place a check next to those statements they thought or believed. It was not surprising that almost every one of the statements were checked.

Many people have now used the list to help identify their wrong thinking, and when asked to check which thoughts they've had, it's not uncommon that many—if not most—of the negative self-statements are marked.

This list should help you understand more of what's going on inside your head.

___I'm worthless.
___I'm a nobody.
___Nothing good will happen to me.
___This is as good as it gets.
___I'm a slut (ho, bitch, whore).

___It's my fault.

___I can't trust myself.

___I can't trust anyone.

___No one can help.

___No one cares.

___I can't do anything right.

___I chose this life.

___I can't make good decisions.

___I'll never change.

___God is impotent(can't help).

___God doesn't care(won't help).

___God doesn't exist.

___Life won't or can't get any better.

___My feelings don't matter.

___Good things won't happen to me.

___I am to blame.

___All I'm good for is sex.

___I must not let things bother me.

___I must hide or ignore my feelings.

___I've got to take care of others.

___I am a bad person.

___I'm stupid.

___Those who say they love or care about me will use and abuse me.

___I'm so ashamed.

___I must be tough and not let things bother me.

___Love always hurts.

___This is what I deserve.

___It's hopeless (the situation).

___I'm helpless.

___I'm hopeless.

____I don't deserve anything good.

____I should have tried harder.

____I should have known better.

____I'll never be good for anything.

____Life will always be bad for me.

My Experience

Place a check next to those lies (above) that you believed and circle those you still believe.

List some of the strongest lies you still believe and refute them (write why they are not true). If this is hard, ask a supportive friend or professional counselor for help.

Reflections

Thoughts, feelings, drawings, notes, or doodles

CHAPTER 15

How We Respond: Symptoms and Behaviors

magine a small local store in your neighborhood. You shop there often and are friendly with the owner. One day, some robbers target that little corner store. They demand all of the money from the owner, who is behind the cash register. After they take the money and grab some expensive items, they beat and kick the owner before leaving. The police and ambulance are summoned. When the police question the owner, they ask questions and make statements such as, "Why didn't you run or fight back? Why didn't you yell and scream at the men and tell them to stop? Why didn't you have a better alarm system? You should have worn protective gear. You should have installed better video surveillance. Why did you leave so much money in the cash box? Don't you have a safe on the premises? You should have known better or tried harder."

Does this scenario sound familiar? It seems crazy, yet this is similar to what happens to those who have been abused. You were harmed. You are the victim. You are confused, yet feel like the accused. You begin to feel the weight of those accusatory comments and the questions cut through your soul. You begin to doubt yourself. You start believing the crazy thoughts. Your self-esteem plummets, and your emotions fluctuate. As you go on these emotional roller coaster rides, you begin acting out and doing things you'd never have done before. Your behavior changes as you wrestle alone with your negative, secret, unhealthy thoughts.

Does that scenario sound familiar? For many, it does, though the progression is different for each person. Those who have been abused act out with unhealthy behaviors resulting from negative internal thoughts and feelings. The accompanying low self-worth, self-blame, and shame that you experience is displayed in your actions and attitudes. Most of these are harmful and self-destructive.

We engage in these damaging behaviors as a way of coping with our internal turmoil. We do these to deaden the emotional pain and to drown out the lies.

I felt so bad about myself, I started drinking and then quickly went to using drugs.

Since I was forced to have sex and didn't have a choice, when I got older I decided that I wanted to be in control, so I began sleeping around with lots of guys.

I'd lie, steal, cheat, do crazy things. I didn't care what happened to me because I felt worthless.

Cutting, eating disorder, suicide attempts—you name it, I did it. I hated myself.

Why Am I Doing This?

Let's take a break for a moment and remember why you're going through this book. Getting it out and facing the effects of the abuse is much, much better than letting it eat you up inside. You may think you have it under control or have good coping skills, but chances are you are just fooling yourself.

Each part of this book takes you on a journey toward the truth about what happened and why you've acted the way you've acted or made the decisions you've made. You are facing the past to improve the future. You *were* the victim but now you are moving from the wounded to the victorious, from the blamed to the brave. You have the courage to hope.

This section, like others, may bring up regrets and remorse. You may need extra time to process the reality of how you may have externalized what was going on inside. Proceed when you feel strong and safe, and have a supportive shoulder to lean on.

Unhealthy Responses and Destructive Behaviors— Our Coping Mechanisms

How do victims act out? What are some of the behaviors, generally unhealthy, you've utilized to cope with all that is going on in your heart and mind? The following statements represent harmful behaviors often exhibited. Some behaviors may be in the past, while you may still be engaging in others.

In an attempt to deal with the internal pain of the abuse:

___I've lied, cheated, and manipulated others.

___I've stolen.

___I've vandalized property or things.

___I ran away.

___I have abused alcohol.

___I've used illegal drugs.

___I've used inhalants or other chemicals.

___I've been depressed and sad for long amounts of time.

___Some people said I was crazy or had bizarre behavior.

___I became promiscuous and slept with a lot of people.

___I've cut myself and done other acts of self-harm or self-mutilation.

___I've developed addictions.

___I've had eating problems or disorders.

___I've had compulsive behavior.

___I've acted and been tough, defiant, and rebellious.

___I've been aggressive and bullied others.

___I've been passive and weak.

___I can be quite impulsive.

___I've had times when I hated myself and had low self-esteem.

___I employ self-deprecation.

___I've had problems with trusting others and with being suspicious.

___I've had problems getting along with others.

___Sometimes I became too clingy or indiscriminate in relationships.

___I've had lots of problems with anger or my temper.

___I developed some sexual addictions: pornography, masturbation, or similar.

___I've had problems with boundaries (co-dependency).

___It has been hard for me to take care of myself (self-protection, self-care).

___I've had multiple physical problems.

___I get sick frequently.

___I've had suicidal behaviors, thoughts, and attempts.

___I've had anxiety or panic attacks.

___I dissociate (tune out, have out-of-body experiences, and/or lose time).

___I've developed imaginary friends.

___I've had school problems (academic and/or achievement).

___I've had trouble making friends and fitting in (social problems).

___I've had problems getting close to people (attachment, bonding).

___I like to help others perhaps more than normal (rescuing others, caretaking).

___I like to be invisible, to withdraw from others, and be detached.

___I sabotage success and expect failure.

___I've been an overachiever, perfectionist.

___I've developed some strange habits.

___I've exercised way too much (excessive exercising).

___Other: _____

___Other: _____

___Other: _____

My Experience

Place an X next to all the unhealthy responses and de-structive behaviors (above) that you engaged in, expe-rienced, or developed in the past. Then, go back and place a circle around those behaviors you are still doing.

Were you encouraged or discouraged by the number of coping behaviors you have engaged in as a result of what happened to you?

Were you encouraged or discouraged, in comparison, by the number of coping behaviors that you still do?

Use the following pages to reflect (write, draw) on what you did to cope—to deaden the deep hurts.

Reflections

Thoughts, feelings, drawings, notes, or doodles

CHAPTER 16

What We Did

In the last chapter, you showed your courage as you identified those unhealthy behaviors and coping mechanisms you used to deaden the pain of what happened. The focus was on what you did to yourself in order to deny or deal with the internal agony. In this chapter, you will once again need to be brave as you look further at what you may have done that directly hurt others. Here, you will also address harmful behaviors, not those you've done to yourself, but those you've done to others.

When we talk about trauma, we usually talk about what was done or what happened *to* victims. But as you heal, you must also look at the deep, dark shameful areas where you yourself may have caused trauma or harm *to others*. While this can be excruciating and difficult, it is needed for healing and recovery. As you share your trauma story, you must include the good, the bad, and the ugly. Otherwise, it is like a malignant growth where surgeons remove only part, but not all of it. Unless you get it all out and tell your entire abuse story, there will still be shame, guilt, and remorse festering inside.

Some of the "shameful" things you did were your way of coping or surviving what was happening to you. While some of these you knew were wrong, you did other things because you didn't know they were wrong. You may have engaged in some activities because you were forced, threatened, coerced, or scammed into doing them.

Whatever the reason, you may have done or participated in activities you are painfully ashamed of. In response, you want to forget the memories, block them out, erase them, or pretend they didn't really happen. You live with deep remorse and regret, wanting to keep the memories buried and locked away.

You may need to confess what you did to someone, ask forgiveness from the person(s), make amends, attempt reconciliation, and/or seek professional or legal advice.

Full healing cannot take place without at some point facing what you have done. If this is too difficult to face now, skip over it, but do come back and finish this section. Don't keep it hidden in the dark, where it will rot and worsen, but bring it into the light and receive freedom from its death-hold grip.

> When I was being abused, I'd often plan how I'd abuse him or someone else.
> He made me do sexual things with my younger brother. I was so little and trusted him. I didn't even know it was wrong. Now, I am so ashamed of what I did.

It became a part of the life we were living: to recruit, beat, and threaten others.

I knew it was wrong, but I wanted to do it and did it anyway. I had a lot of anger in me.

When I finally got it out and told someone how ashamed I felt about what I'd done, I was so glad I did because he didn't judge or condemn me.

I always tried to justify what I did but I am so thankful for the forgiveness I've received from God and from one of the people I hurt.

My Experience

Place a check next to those things you did or in which you were a participant. This list is not complete, so please add other areas in which you may have caused harm or trauma to others.

___Lied to family or a close friend

___Lied—to the police, judge, social worker, etc.

___Stolen

___Recruited someone to provide sex for someone else

___Beaten someone up (fists, kicks, etc.); physically assaulted or injured someone

___Killed an animal

___Killed or helped someone kill another person

___Coerced someone into hurting someone else

___Held someone down while others raped or beat her or him

___Sexually abused others

___Injured someone with an object: knife, belt, bottle, stick, whip, etc.

___Given drugs to others

___Sold drugs

___Put foreign objects inside someone's body (mouth, anus, vagina, ears)

___Participated in a group/gang illegal activity (stealing, rape, physical assault, etc.)

___Forced a child to do something to or for you (sexual or otherwise)

___Talked someone into doing something they clearly didn't want to do

___Vandalized or destroyed someone else's property or possession

___Other: _____

___Other: _____

What I Did

___I've done some things that have hurt others.

___I still feel ashamed about it.

___I wish I could undo it all.

___Now looking back, I think I did those things:

    ___To numb the pain I felt inside

    ___To survive, cope

    ___Because I had such rage inside

    ___To hurt others like I felt hurt

    ___Because I didn't know it was wrong

    ___Because I was threatened, forced, or coerced into doing them

    ___Other: _____

    ___Other: _____

What I Need to Do

___Confess to someone what I did

___Ask forgiveness and/or seek reconciliation with the person

___Make amends, provide compensation to the person

___Seek professional help (therapy, legal advice, or other)

Reflections

Thoughts, feelings, drawings, notes, or doodles

The Ongoing Challenges

"The best way out is always through."
-ROBERT FROST

CHAPTER 17

How We Feel about the Abuser

Some people I've worked with have intense emotions about the person or persons who hurt and harmed them. I'm told of the powerful rage or the compassionate, forgiving love.

There are others, however, who seem indifferent. While on their healing journeys, they seldom talk about the abuser. The topic is rarely addressed. They don't know and they don't care where the person is or what's become of him or her. Or so it seems. Many just don't want to "go there" because it's too distressing to discuss. Others just want to forget completely about the abuser, as if he or she didn't exist. They dislike the topic of the abuser.

Here, however, you're being asked to look deeply into the recesses of your heart and identify your feeling toward the abuser. Though distasteful, this is another step toward your desired destination of being free from

BECCA C. JOHNSON, PHD.

the grasp of the lingering effects abuse has had in and on your life.

Anger, love, pity, compassion, betrayal, and hatred are some of the many feelings you may have felt toward your offender(s). Some of these emotions are experienced at the same time, even though they may seem opposite to each other. In the chapter *How We Feel,* we defined ambivalence as having simultaneous, contradictory (oppositional) feelings toward a person, object, or behavior—such as love and hate, attraction and repulsion, enjoyment and disgust.

This may well describe what you experienced. While you may hate the abuse, you may love the abuser. Or you may be disgusted, yet may have enjoyed the attention or bodily sensations of the abuse. You may feel like you must honor and respect the person, yet feel only pity.

Most people assume you should feel only hatred and anger toward your offender, and might even encourage you to do so. Yet that pressure to feel a certain way can make you feel uncomfortable, angry, and misunderstood. When your feelings are different or in contrast to what other, well-meaning people are telling you to feel, it may cause you to shut down and clam up.

Ambivalence brings confusion and uncertainty. Inside it feels like you're going crazy. You try to make sense of the simultaneous and contradictory feelings and beliefs, but are left feeling disoriented and filled with self-doubt.

It is not unusual to have positive feelings toward the offender, especially when the relationship involved trauma bonding or betrayal trauma. In the midst of the trauma, the victim feels responsible for, and/or dependent upon, the perpetrator, who displays kindnesses. When offenders proclaim, "I love you," it adds to the confusion and mixed emotions victims experience.

Feelings and attitudes toward abusers often change as time passes and healing occurs. Some survivors report feeling love, then hatred, then pity, then compassion. Others, progress through feeling anger, betrayal, and forgiveness. As the abuse is explored and exposed, you may find yourself moving through these varied sentiments in different ways at different times.

I loved him, yet hated him. I felt so betrayed.

I hated what was happening, but it was the only time I got any attention.

I kept trying to earn his love, even though I hated how he belittled me.

What I thought was love was just my desperate need for belonging.

I used to think I was going crazy. My feelings toward him shifted like a pendulum, back and forth. One minute, I couldn't stand him, and the next minute, I couldn't wait to see him.

My Experience

(Check as many as apply)
At first, my feelings toward the abuser were_____.
___love   ___hatred   ___pity
___betrayal   ___friendship   ___anger
___compassion   ___other: _____

Later, I felt _____ toward the abuser.
___love   ___hatred   ___pity
___betrayal   ___friendship   ___anger
___compassion   ___forgiveness   ___other:_____

Now, my feelings toward the abuser are_____.
___love   ___hatred   ___pity
___betrayal   ___friendship   ___anger
___compassion   ___forgiveness   ___other: _____

___ I choose not to feel anything toward the abuser.

Reflections

Thoughts, feelings, drawings, notes, or doodles

CHAPTER 18

What About Forgiveness?

The word *forgiveness* can be quite an emotionally charged one. Many victims adamantly state:

I refuse to ever forgive the person who abused me.
I've forgiven him in my head, but I'm still working on forgiving him in my heart.
I've forgiven the person and moved on, but I still struggle with forgiving myself!

I was trying to explain the concept of forgiveness to a group of women who had been horrifically and multiply abused and exploited. One of the women asked, "Do I have to forgive?"

I fumbled for words, talking about the negative effects on ourselves of not forgiving. "When we don't forgive, we are the ones who suffer. When we hang on to hate, we become bitter." Another woman in the group then summed it up beautifully, "Unforgiveness is like drinking poison and expecting the other person to die."

Let's be clear, forgiveness does not mean that you must let those who hurt you back into your life. You do not have to spend time together, be friends again, have coffee, or go on holidays together—unless you so choose. You can choose whether to have any future relationship, but as many victims and professionals would agree, "We don't have a choice of whether to forgive. We must. If we don't, we stay stuck in our past and only hurt ourselves."

I like what one person shared with me, "I've forgiven him for what he did to me, but I won't leave him alone with my children." A pastor once told me, "Did you know that the Bible commands us to 'love one another' and to 'forgive,' but it does not command us to trust one another, only to trust God?" Forgiveness is needed but trust is optional.

When you don't forgive, you are the one to suffer. When anger and hurt are not resolved, you run the risk of becoming a cynical, bitter grudge keeper. Lingering anger and unforgiveness generally morph into heart-crushing bitterness or uncontrollable rage.

Who Do We Forgive?

When we talk about the importance of forgiveness, however, we aren't just referring to the abuser. There may be other people you need to forgive. Maybe it is a non-offending, unprotecting parent or the parent who knew about or suspected the abuse but said nothing. Maybe it's the adult you told who ignored or minimized what you shared—and did nothing. Maybe it's the helper (teacher, social worker, law enforcement) who didn't follow up on the concern. And of course, you need to forgive yourself.

Do you remember the chapter examining our often misguided anger? Many feel more anger toward themselves or others related to their abuse than toward the abuser! For your own sake, you need to work on forgiving those who hurt you or didn't protect you.

When George came in to counseling, he emphatically told me during that first session, "There's no way I'm ever going to forgive her for what she did to me." As time progressed, I listened to his deep hurt, verbally vomited week after week. During our times together, he also shared his deep self-hatred for not having stopped the abuse and for not doing something about it. When we finally broached the topic of forgiveness, he restated what he'd said that first session.

He was surprised when I asked, "But what about yourself? Are you willing to forgive yourself?"

It is imperative that you forgive yourself. You've blamed and beaten yourself up again and again. You thought to yourself, "Why didn't I…" or "I should have…" or "If only I…" Now is the time to forgive yourself.

What are the potential benefits of forgiveness? "Forgiveness yields good things—peace, happiness, health, reconciliation…people who forgave also tended to have fewer mental problems…[Research supports] the power of forgiveness to heal the mind, body, and spirit."[19]

What happens when you don't forgive? Physically, you may experience ulcers, high blood pressure, tense muscles, and difficulties with sleep. Emotionally, you may develop bitterness and a sense of being unsettled or anxious. Socially, relationships can be adversely affected by your inner anger. And spiritually, your faith suffers as you feel distant from, or disappointed in, God.

What Is and Isn't Forgiveness

Forgiveness is willfully choosing to release the hurt and the desire for revenge. It's a choice, not a feeling. I've heard it said, "When it comes to forgiveness, you have to choose it." This means that you consciously make the decision to forgive, even when you don't feel like it. It is making up your mind to do something and then daily facing the challenges of living out that decision. You don't wait until you feel it, you determine to do it, regardless of your fluctuating emotions. You willingly say, "I forgive," with no timeline or pressure for your heart to catch up.

Let's look at what forgiveness is and isn't.[20]

Forgiveness IS...

- An attempt to let go of past hurts and anger.
- A decision not to let the past determine the future.
- A powerful way to neutralize volatile emotions.
- A choice.
- A step toward becoming more compassionate.
- An amazing way to move forward.
- Necessary.

Forgiveness is NOT...

- Condoning the behavior.
- Forgetting what happened.
- Restoring trust in the person.
- Agreeing to reconcile.
- Doing the person a favor.
- Easy.

My Experience

I need to:

Check as many as apply

___Forgive the abuser
___Forgive my parents

___Forgive someone who didn't help
___Forgive myself

and...

___I refuse to forgive those who hurt me.
___I refuse to forgive those who didn't protect or help me (parent, others).
___I want to forgive those who hurt me, but it's hard.
___I will forgive, but I won't forget or trust the people again.
___I do not want reconciliation with the offender(s).
___I know I need to forgive myself, but it's hard to do.
___I choose to forgive the abuser.
___I choose to forgive those involved who didn't help.
___I choose to forgive myself.
___I _____

Reflections

Thoughts, feelings, drawings, notes, or doodles

CHAPTER 19

What Lingers About the Abuse: Memories and Triggers

I was supervising a support group for women who have been sexually exploited. After our time together, one of the women asked to speak with me, saying that the program director had encouraged her to share her concerns with me. Once we were alone, she blurted out, "You remind me so much of the woman who abused and used me for many, many years." She continued, "You are my biggest trigger."

At first, I was taken off guard, not knowing what to say, and then the words came suddenly and with energy. "Then I'm all the more impressed that you could participate in group today with me sitting right next to you. That's incredible that you could overcome those negative feelings and continue on in group. You shared some insightful and helpful comments. You are amazing!"

By the look on her face, I could tell that she didn't expect that response. She paused for a moment, then replied, "I'm glad I shared it with you. I think I'm over it now."

A friend shared that, after 20 years, her heart still leaps to her throat whenever she sees a red Mustang. "Every time I see that car, my heart starts pounding and I can't breathe. That was the car my abuser drove. Whenever I saw his car, I knew something bad was going to happen."

Another person identified his fear of dogs as stemming from his abuse. Whenever there was screaming in the house and he was being beaten, the neighbor's dog would bark loud and long. "To this day, I still get nervous and scared whenever I hear a dog bark. I feel like I'm in imminent danger. It's an automatic reaction I can't control, like Pavlov's salivating dog."

The abuse you experienced is etched in your mind. Memories linger. Some of the memories have come and gone, some come without any reaction, but others are accompanied by strong negative emotions, bodily sensations, or flashbacks. You may experience shortness of breath, tense muscles, an anxiety attack, the sensation of reliving the event, digestive problems, and more. Even if you've worked through the abuse and feel closure, you may still be haunted by certain reminders.

Triggers

Many of these memories developed into *triggers,* or instant reminders of the abuse. These can bring unpleasant or traumatizing thoughts, feelings, and reactions, or they can lead to a flashback, in which the trauma event is experienced, once again, as if it were recurring.

> *I get sick to my stomach whenever I smell that certain aftershave cologne.*
>
> *A man walked down the street with a particular kind of hat on, and I lost it. I didn't remember until then that the abuser wore the same kind of hat.*
>
> *If my partner touches me a certain way, I freeze and start to panic.*
>
> *Sometimes it's still hard for me to look a blond-haired, blue-eyed person in the eyes.*
>
> *I hate red curtains, futons, wood floors, or holes in the wall!*
>
> *Loud music and diesel trucks set me off.*
>
> *Dreams are my trigger—when I have a nightmare about him or what happened.*

There are certain people, places, events, and things, as well as certain sights, sounds, tastes, touches, and smells that can trigger our negative memories. Identifying them can be a challenge, but well worth the effort. It's hard to fight a ghost you can't see. Recognizing these intruders enables us to develop defensive and offensive strategies to help in our healing.

If you're ready to stop shadowboxing, and face the memories and their accompanying triggers, you'll need to write down as much as you can remember about the sights, sounds, touches, tastes, and smells surrounding the abuse. Once you've identified these, it's much easier to identify triggers that have developed in your life as a result of what happened.

My Experience

Memories

Write down any memories related to the abuse, in the following areas.

When I was being abused, I remember:

Sights: _____

    (colorful wallpaper, dark room, trees outside, old clothes)

Sounds: _____

    (dog barking, music playing, loud breathing, teapot whistle)

Touch: _____

    (soft baby blanket, facial hair, rough hands, wet skin)

Tastes: _____

    (blood, coffee, saliva, semen)

Smells: _____

(aftershave, vomit, sweat, garlic)

My Triggers

Now that you have bravely identified elements of the intrusive memories, let's recognize what people, places, things, events, emotions, or behaviors still activate unhealthy responses for you.

Using the abuse memories you just listed (sights, sounds, touches, tastes, and smells), make a list of those specific people, places, things, dreams, events, and/or behaviors that trigger negative reactions.

Reflections

Thoughts, feelings, drawings, notes, or doodles

CHAPTER 20

What Helps and What Hinders Our Healing

realized years ago that I can't watch movies about injustice. I get too upset and find it hard to sleep. I relive the negative events in the movie over and over again. And forget movies or documentaries on disasters, tragedies, or horror—not me, never, no. It's not good for me. Similarly, I've learned that I can't watch or read the news. It's too discouraging and depressing. I work with people who have been horribly and multiply traumatized, so I don't want to invite any more trauma and bad news into my life. It's too much and too hard. It took me years to realize this, but now I have some clear boundaries, self-imposed limitations, and healthy avoidance areas.

In the last chapter, we talked about triggers developed directly from your abuse memories. Here, we talk about anything and everything that may negatively affect you. Like triggers, we want to expose them so we can avoid them. Conversely, we will also acknowledge those people, places, and things that bring joy and peace to your life. What are those things that invigorate, enliven, refresh, encourage, uplift, or calm you? Pinpoint them, do them, and do them often.

You're nearing the end of this journey of healing from your abusive past. It's time to make a personal list of what helps (or has helped) in this learning-growing-healing-helping process and what gets in the way or hinders your progress.

What Hinders?

Factors such as self-blame, worry, being around the abuser or your family, being alone, horror movies, reading stories of abuse and exploitation, or drugs and alcohol can hinder your progress. What obstacles—people, places, things, moods, events, or experiences—set you back?

What Helps?

What helps you along your healing journey? It can be prayer, journaling, solitude, listening to music, exercise, hot baths, jogging, or talking with friends. Or it could be facing the abuse, sharing your story, helping others, or volunteering with children and other life-giving, helpful, restorative activities.

For many, your faith and beliefs have been foundational and essential in your healing journey. This hope-giving, soul-nourishing, and peace-infusing faith has been the cornerstone of healing that holds everything together. Whether or not you profess a religious belief or acknowledge a higher power, know that countless individuals have found God to be the main source of strength and the key to healing on this weary journey.

For some, solitude brings peace, while for others, anxiety. Some like to journal and write, others prefer activity and exercise. Some gravitate toward art, music, or dance; others to parties and gatherings, opportunities for social interaction. What helps will be specific to each person. Your list of what helps and hinders will be unique to you.

Identifying what helps and what hinders your personal growth is important as you seek to move ahead. As stated, your list will be different and unique, a reflection of what works for you individually. Your goal is to engage more fully and consciously in those things that help you move forward. The following is an example:

Things That Help	Things That Hinder
+Listening to/playing music	-Thinking the problem is my fault
+My faith in God	-My 'family obligations and duty'
+My determination and perseverance	-The abuser's denial
+Talking with supportive friends	-No money for therapy
+Going for a walk, a run, or a swim	-People's impatience or pity
+Dancing or moving around	-Seeing my Dad

+Writing in my journal or doing something artsy
+Playing with my pet
+Hitting a pillow or using a foam bat
+Taking a shower or bath
+Muscle relaxation and focused breathing
+Trauma Release Exercises (TRE)

-My porn/masturbation addiction
-Walking along the riverfront
-Poor sleep, being tired
-Wondering if I'll ever feel better

The Role of Relaxation

While each person has different activities that harm or help, relaxation techniques are highly recommended for everyone. Trauma recovery models encourage the use of relaxation methods. These techniques or activities can include focused deep breathing, progressive muscle relaxation, guided imagery, yoga, and mindfulness (meditation, centering, grounding).

When intrusive, anxiety-producing memories invade one's mind, doing one or more of these relaxation techniques can help. Whether you call it anxiety management, stress reduction, or self-calming activities, you are encouraged to learn, identify, and use whichever methods work best for you. The following are some of the more commonly used or recommended relaxation techniques (with an overly simplified explanation of each):

- *Progressive muscle relaxation* — tightening and then releasing various muscles throughout the body.
- *Deep breathing* — focused, controlled breathing (somewhat similar to that used in childbirth).
- *Meditation/mindfulness/grounding*—intentional focus on being present in the present.
- *Tension and trauma release exercises* (TRE) — facilitation of the release of therapeutic muscle tremors (activating a neurogenic, shaking response).
- *Guided imagery*—imagining self at a safe and peaceful place, recalling the calming sights, sounds, and smells.
- *Yoga, tai chi* — gentle stretching and posed exercises for body and mind.
- *Body massage* — for overall physical health, improves circulation, and releases muscle tension.

My Experience

What *hinders* my growth? What is harmful for me? (Make a list as things come to mind.) Here are some obstacles (people, places, things, emotions, events, habits, etc.) that hinder my progress:

What *helps* me grow, feel better, and move forward? Here are some people, places, things, emotions, events, habits, and similar that help my progress:

What Helps Me Relax, Calm Down, Feel Better, and Eliminate Stress?

Check those (and add more) that help you:

___Take a shower   ___Play with children
___Take a bubble bath   ___Dance or movement
___Go swimming   ___Play with animals
___Read a book   ___Cook and eat
___Go for a walk   ___Talk with a friend
___Go for a run   ___Hang out with friends
___Exercise   ___Work
___Write a poem   ___Watch a movie or TV
___Write in my journal   ___Create something/art
___Listen to music   ___Sew
___Play games or puzzles   ___Clean
___Help others   ___Meditation/mindfulness

___Read my Bible   ___Play music (guitar, piano)
___Pray   ___Take a nap / sleep
___Hit a pillow
___Other:_____

Reflections

Thoughts, feelings, drawings, notes, or doodles

CHAPTER 21

What About the Future?

*Sometimes I feel like giving up, other times I want to stay
and fight.*
*I finally feel ready to face the abuse, get some help and
move on.*
*Sometimes, I scream into my pillow, sometimes I shout
for joy. I take one day at a time.*

"Take one day at a time" is good advice. We have good days and we have bad, hard, discouraging days. I don't doubt that the good days will eventually outnumber the hard days for you as you face the painful past. I've experienced it in my own life, and I have seen it in the lives of many who struggled with getting out of bed, putting one foot ahead of another, and moving forward. I believe that some of the biggest lies are, "Life won't get better" and "This is as good as it gets." The truth is, life does get better—the pain eases, the grief lessens, the anger subsides, and the anxiety dissipates. There is happiness after sadness, peace after the storm, and joy after grief.

The future holds more possibilities, more plans to be made. Old dreams are rediscovered and new ones emerge. Hope pushes doubt out and then moves in to stay. The future holds more potential than fears, more prospects than failures.

On those tough days, cling to *hope* and don't let go. Keep on keeping on. Persevere. Be determined not to give up. Commit to forward motion.

As you plan for the future, you need to evaluate your present state. Where are you in the healing process? What are you thinking and feeling?

Current Thoughts and Feelings

I want to *(check as many as apply)*:

___Move on.

___Get the pain out.

___Get counseling.

___Turn to God.

___Stop using.

___Toughen up.

___Tell someone.

___Cry and scream.

___Put the abuse in perspective.

___Share my story.

___Report what happened.

___Help others like me.

___Forget it ever happened.

___Feel better.

___Get rid of my intense anger.

___Get rid of my addictions.

___Forgive.

___Other: _____.

___Other: _____.

Are you feeling hopeful that healing is possible? Do you already sense more inner strength and determination?

Or are you feeling overwhelmed and defeated, like you'll never be able to overcome the trauma of the abuse?

If you're the latter, don't give up, and don't give in. You can overcome the pain of your past, but you must be willing to face it.

The goal is to move from victim to survivor to over-comer to "thriver." Surround yourself with safe people. Face the trauma head on, remembering to be patient and gracious with yourself.

My Experience

Return to this chapter's first list of possible current thoughts and feelings, checking those with which you identify. Then, add any of your own thoughts, plans, and/or goals.

What I Choose to Believe Now

Now that you've learned about abuse and unhelpful thinking, you can now replace the lies and choose healthy beliefs such as these:

___*It wasn't my fault.*

___*I can heal from my past.*

___*I was not responsible for what happened.*

___*The pain will not last forever.*

___*I was only partially responsible.*

___*I choose not to believe the lies in my head.*

___*I am going to share my story.*

___*I am okay. I am not worthless or damaged.*

___*I can learn to overcome and even to thrive.*

___*I can help others. I have something to offer.*

Reflections

Thoughts, feelings, drawings, notes, or doodles

CHAPTER 22

Future Possibilities and Pursuits

A teacher, stylist, chef, nurse, engineer, social worker, pastor, speaker, writer, business owner—what do you want to do?

The abuse that happened to you does not have to determine who you are—your identity or your future. Yes, it was part of your life, but it should never define the entirety of your life. You have potential and possibilities. You have strengths and abilities.

Identity Change

For most of us, we find our identity in who we are (our personality), what we like (our preferences), what we own (possessions), our smarts (intelligence), what we're good at (skills and abilities), or in our looks (appearance). Each of us prefers or leans toward one of these areas as we define our identity.

When I began to see Anna in my counseling office, it became apparent quite quickly that her identity was wrapped up in her abilities in a particular area. She said, "There's one thing I'm good at, perhaps the only thing I'm good at." She was only 19 years old at the time, but talked like a person well versed and experienced. She shared, "I am good at sex."

As her story unraveled, from her early childhood, for many years, she'd been multiply abused by numerous family members. In high school, with her feelings of self-worth in a bottomless pit, she became promiscuous. She felt that being sexually active with many of the boys would gain her recognition and attention. It did. She was known as the girl to go to if you wanted to have a "good time." She shared, "I was forced to have sex against my will for so many years, so I decided I was now going to take charge of that part of my life."

As our sessions progressed, however, Anna shared of the deep sadness, shame, self-hatred, and self-blame. She confessed that she didn't like her sex-oriented identity. She wanted a new identity.

How does someone change his or her identity? How do you change how you view yourself and how others view you? What does one need to do for that to happen?

We talked about the hopes and dreams she'd had as a child. We identified what she enjoyed doing—music, art, dance, sports, and journaling. We focused on the possibilities and not the problems.

Then, like a constrained caterpillar, seemingly forever bound in a cocoon, a beautiful butterfly burst forth. Anna proudly announced one day, "I am a writer." Continuing on, "I love to write, to express thoughts and feelings in written form, to communicate. I am a writer." Her declaration denounced the former identity she'd incorporated. She was free of the hated identity and embraced her newly discovered one. Renewed energy spurred her on to write and write and refine her craft. Anna is a writer now—and she's good at it.

Do not let the pain of the past define your identity or determine your destiny.

The abuse is part of your life story, but it's only a chapter. It's not the entire account, nor is it the end of the tale.

As you heal, you will find that long-forgotten dreams and plans re-emerge, and new ones take shape. You are like the caterpillar coming forth from the cocoon. It must struggle to free itself (a necessary process) in order to become the free-to-fly, beautiful butterfly. You too must struggle to free yourself from the negative effects of the abuse that have wrapped and trapped you. As you break free, you are free to hope and dream again.

- Do you have dreams and hopes?
- What do you want to do?
- What did you once dream of doing, becoming?
- Do you want to volunteer to help children, animals, other survivors, victims of domestic violence, at-risk youth, or those with special needs?
- Where do you dream of going or what do you dream of seeing?

- If you could be or do anything, what would it be?
- What do you need to do to make some of your long-forgotten, but still wanted dreams come true?
- Where do you hope to be and what do you plan to be doing five years from now?

My Experience

My Future Hopes and Plans

I would like to _____

I would like to study/work/do _____

I would like to help _____

I would like to meet _____

I would like to finish _____

I would like to go _____

I hope to be in a relationship with someone who _____
_____

I would like to get better at _____
_____

If I have children, I would _____
_____

I have a dream to _____
_____

I would like to be someone who _____
_____

I plan to _____
_____

Here are some of my hopes, dreams, and plans for the future: *(Use additional paper or a journal, if needed.)*

Reflections

Thoughts, feelings, drawings, notes, or doodles

The Healing Story

"Success is the sum of small efforts,
repeated day in and day out."
—ROBERT COLLIER

CHAPTER 23

Telling My Abuse Story

We began this book learning that telling one's trauma story is key in the healing process. If you want to get on with your life, you have to get it out. Keeping it in is similar to leaving an operable malignant tumor inside without saying yes to a surgery. Abuse survivors have repeatedly said that this process of sharing the details of their abuse story, though scary and unwanted, was key in turning the corner for their healing.

> *After sharing, which I didn't want to do, I felt lighter, like a heavy weight had been lifted off my soul.*
>
> *I was not looking forward to telling what happened, but trusted the counselor when she said it would be good for me. I am so glad I did. What a relief I felt, not because I got through it, but because I felt better about myself and what happened.*
>
> *I'm so glad I didn't bail on doing this. It's so important to not keep it inside!*

By going through these chapters and completing the checklists and questions, you've shared the pieces of your story. In this chapter, we want to put it all together, and it is my hope that when you are ready, you can use this chapter as a tool to share your story with another person.

As already shared, it is not uncommon to be abused at various times by different people. Although your heart might resist going through this final storytelling, you are encouraged to make a few copies of these pages so that you can complete them for *each* abusive relationship you experienced. It's not enjoyable, but can be very valuable in your journey to hope and healing.

My Abuse Story

(Becca C. Johnson, PhD, 2010)

When I was _____ years old, I was abused by *(name)* _____, my *(relationship, chapter 6)* _____. It happened most of the time in or at *(locations, chapter 7)* _____ and _____.

I experienced the following types of abuse *(chapter 3, check all that apply)* ____physical ____sexual ____emotional/verbal abuse ____neglect

Write or describe what happened, using as much detail as possible. (Use additional paper as needed.)

This is what happened:_____

_____

_____

_____

_____

Most often, it happened *(time of day, certain day of week)*

_____.

It happened this often: ___once ___once a month ___ every week ___daily ___# times total

The abuse went on for ____# ___years ___ months ___weeks ___days

Who else was in the area (house, building) when you were being molested?

_____.

I suspect_____*(name)* knew that something was going on.

I know_____ *(name)* saw something going on and knew about the abuse.

I think the perpetrator may have also abused _____
_____.

My Reaction
(Chapter 8)
Fight Flight (Flee) Freeze
Check all that apply:

___ I still believe I could or should have responded differently.

___ I have carried much guilt and shame from believing that I didn't respond as I should have.

___ Now I know that it wasn't wrong or shameful to freeze.

___ Now I know that it is common to comply.

___ I didn't react because I didn't know it was wrong.

___ I didn't react because I thought I didn't have a choice.

___ Other: _____

My Thoughts and Beliefs
(Chapter 9)
I realize that I've tended to _____
(minimize, rationalize, deny, blocked, mislabel) what happened to me. When the abuse happened, I thought:

_____
_____.

Keeping Silent?
(Chapter 11)
I kept silent (I didn't tell anyone) because *(refer to the long list in chapter 11)*

_____   _____

_____   _____

_____   _____

My Feelings About the Abuse
(Chapter 12)
Check the feelings from the list below that you have felt about the abuse. Circle the feelings that you continue to feel.

___Angry   ___Hopeless or depressed

___Anxious, worried   ___Loved

___Aroused   ___Numb

___Betrayed   ___Powerless

___Blamed   ___Sad

___Confused (ambivalent)   ___Scared, fearful

___Deceived   ___Shame

___Dirty   ___Sneaky

___Embarrassed   ___Special

___Excited   ___Stuck or trapped

___Guilty   ___Stupid

___Helpless   ___Other: _____

Where I Direct My Anger
(Chapter 13)
Check all that apply:

___ I still blame myself.

___ I tend to excuse the abuser more than I excuse myself.

___ I tend to direct my anger at myself.

___ I need to redirect my anger at the abuser.

___ I need to not be so hard on myself.

___ I need to forgive myself.

___ I am angry at _____. *(God, parent, law enforcement, teacher, other.)*

What We Think
(Refer to the long list in chapter 14.)
    Here are the *lies* I most believe:

_____   _____

_____   _____

_____   _____

_____   _____

_____   _____

_____

Here's What I Did to Cope with What Happened
(Refer to the long list in chapter 15 of harmful behaviors and write down those you most commonly used.)

What I Did
(Chapter 16)
Check all that apply:

___I've done some things that have hurt others.
___I wish I could undo it all.
___I still feel ashamed about it.
___Now looking back, I think I did those things to others:
    ___Because I was threatened, forced, or coerced into
        doing bad things to others.
    ___To numb the pain I felt.
    ___To survive, to cope.
    ___Because I had such rage inside.
    ___To hurt others like I felt hurt.
    ___Because I didn't know it was wrong.
    ___Other: _____.

Feelings Toward the Abuser
(Chapter 17)
Mark all that apply:
    √ = *before the abuse*   X = *during the abuse*   0 = *now*

___Love	___Hatred	___Anger
___Betrayal	___Friendship	___Other:___
___Compassion	___Pity	

Forgiving?
(Chapter 18)
Check all that apply:

___I refuse to forgive those who hurt me.

___I refuse to forgive those who didn't protect or help me.

___I want to forgive those who hurt me, but it's hard.

___I will forgive, but I won't forget nor trust the people again.

___I do not want reconciliation with the offender(s).

___I need to forgive myself.

___I_____.

Helpful Decisions and Future Plans
(Chapter 20-22)

___I will strive to remember to do those things that help me to heal.

___I will seek to avoid those things that make me feel worse.

___I will seek help from others (friends, family, and/or professionals) to help in this healing journey.

*These are the people, places, things, and events that **help me feel better**:*

I want to *(check as many as apply):*
(Chapter 21)

___Move on   ___Help others like me
___Get the pain out   ___Forget it ever happened
___Get counseling   ___Feel better
___Turn to God   ___Get rid of my intense
___Stop using   anger
___Toughen up   ___Get rid of my sex
___Tell someone   addiction
___Cry and scream   ___Forgive
___Share my story   ___Other: _____
___Report what happened   ___Other: _____

I don't want what happened to me to determine my future possibilities. I will pursue my future plans, dreams, and goals *(chapter 21).*

Here are some of my future plans, hopes, and dreams: *(chapter 22)*

CHAPTER 24

Sharing with a Safe Person

N ow that you've put together your story, you should share it with someone. Trauma healing models encourage you to *tell* your story to a safe, nonjudgmental, supportive, caring person. Getting it out *and* sharing it is a key step on your healing journey.

Kira didn't want to tell her story to anyone besides me. The counseling office was like a quarantined, safe bubble and she didn't want others to know her story. I told her that sharing her story with another person is considered very helpful in the healing process. She looked doubtful, but fortunately, had grown to trust me.

We discussed whom she wanted to invite and which story to share from her many traumas. She chose a safe person and "the least horrible trauma." After she told of her abuse and the person left, she agreed, "That *was* good for me. I was trembling while I was talking, but now I feel great. I didn't think it would feel like this *(so good)* to tell someone else."

Like many others, Kira questioned the benefit of sharing her story. Most bemoan, "Do I have to? Is it really necessary?"

To this I reply, "Yes." Trauma research confirms that telling your story to one or more people assists in healing and can bring a sense of closure.

Before you take this brave step and share your story with someone you trust, you'll want to make sure the person is safe—that he or she is emotionally safe for you.

Here are a few guidelines for helping you choose the person with whom to share your story.

Is the person:

___A good listener?

___Caring?

___Capable of listening to tough stuff?

___Able to listen and not get overly emotional?

___Able to keep focused on you and not have it become about him or her?

___Not judgmental, blaming nor critical?

___Able to not blame themselves for what happened?

___Able to keep confidentiality (not tell anyone)?

___Supportive of you, who you are, and your healing journey?

If you are unsure of any of the above with the person you are thinking about, you might want to reconsider and choose a different person. Sharing your story is hard enough without feeling like you need to take care of the person, worry about confidentiality, or their reaction.

Sharing My Experience

I am sharing my story with: *(name)* _____
Relationship: *(friend, family, mentor)*_____
Date shared: _____

Note that if you are seeing a therapist, coach, or mentor, you can begin by sharing your story with him or her. But do not stop there. It is strongly recommended that you share your story with someone else—a friend or relative—someone outside of a mentor, coach, or client-therapist relationship.

Writing Letters

Sharing your story is not the same as writing a letter to the one who hurt you or to a parent or caregiver who didn't protect you or know about it. Some have found writing a letter to be helpful in their healing journey, but it is certainly optional and must be undertaken with great care and support. Most shred or burn the letters, but if you decide to send it, make sure you are aware of, and prepared for, the possible repercussions. While many find writing the letters to be a powerful healing exercise, others find it too painful or irrelevant.

You may want to do this even though the person is dead or unknown. Should you give the letters, discard, or burn them,—discuss the pros and cons with your support people. (Example letters are included in appendices B and C: *Letter to the Abuser* and *Letter to a Non-offending Caregiver.*)

Reflections

Thoughts, feelings, drawings, notes, or doodles

CHAPTER 25

What's Next

f you've shared your story with someone else, congratulations. You are courageous! You have loosened the chains of your past and cast them off. You are free from the shackles that have bound you for too long.

If you've suffered abuse and you've read the book, but not yet completed the checklists, questions, or shared your story, that's okay—*for now.* I would encourage you to return to complete them later when you're feeling safe and supported.

My desire is that this book has been beneficial, whether you read it to *learn,* to *heal,* or to *help* others.

If you used this book for your own *healing,* then you've completed the many exercises, questions, and checklists. Through the agony and aches, grief and guilt, sadness and shame, you have faced the ferocious and emerged victorious. No longer a victim, you are a genuine survivor. Go live and enjoy life more fully, unencumbered by past burdens and barriers.

Triggers from your past may continue to bother you, and you may want to seek counseling. Through it all, you have gained strength and control. You will still face challenges in life—this is normal as we face the ups and downs of life.

My prayer is that you will be more at peace with yourself. Remember, don't let your past trauma define who you are or determine your destiny. Look to the future with possibilities and to yourself with grace.

Dr. Becca

About the Author

D r. Becca Johnson is a recognized and respected leader with a passion to help the hurting heal. With over 25 years of experience as a licensed psychologist she brings a unique perspective and set of skills that enable a holistic approach to recovery and restoration for survivors of sexual abuse and exploitation.

Currently, Dr. Johnson serves as the International Training Director for Rescue:Freedom International, a non-profit organization that empowers the rescue and restoration of those trapped in sexual slavery and prevents exploitation.

As a sought after expert, she has provided training for those working with victims of sexual abuse, human trafficking, and exploitation. She trains on topics such as trauma care and recovery to programs globally and has provided training for International Justice Mission (IJM), Shared Hope International, Salvation Army and many other organizations. Last year alone she trained over 2,000 social workers, care providers and clinicians from 45 countries in workshops and clinics held in 14 countries.

Dr. Johnson is the clinical advisor for Engedi Refuge, a recovery home for sexually exploited women. She has provided individual and group therapy as well as training for their staff and volunteers. Since 2006, she has consulted and trained on sex-trafficking victim aftercare for Agape International Mission (AIM), both in the United States and abroad.

Becca is actively involved with Royal Family KIDS (in both North and South America) and TRAC (Teen Reach Adventure Camp) - camp, club and mentoring programs for abused and neglected children and youth in the foster care system.

Dr. Johnson is the author of books on child abuse (*For Their Sake: Recognizing, Responding and Reporting Child Abuse*, ACA, 1991), guilt (*Good Guilt, Bad Guilt*, IVP, 1996) and anger (*Overcoming Emotions that Destroy*, co-authored with Chip Ingram, Baker Books, 2008).

Becca and her husband live in Bellingham, Washington (USA). They have five grown children.

APPENDIX A

Possible Indicators of Abuse

Becca C. Johnson, 1992[21]

Those working with minors are mandated to report child abuse, not just when told, but also when suspected. Too often, too many people neglect to report—doubting or minimizing their observations.

The following checklist, developed over 20 years ago, includes *possible* indicators of abuse. That is, children and adolescents experience many of these, yet are not abused. Caution must be given when using this list. It is meant to provide insight and assistance in the identification of child abuse when numerous indicators are observed together. Only a few items (*), in and of themselves, are stronger possible indicators of child abuse.

Sexual Abuse—Behavioral Indicators:

___1. Reluctance to change clothes in front of others.
___2. Withdrawn
___3. *Sexualized behavior toward adults or other children, unusual sexual behavior, and/or knowledge beyond that which is common for the particular developmental age.
___4. Poor peer relationships
___5. Either avoids or seeks out adults
___6. Pseudomature
___7. Manipulative
___8. Self-conscious
___9. Problems with authority and rules.
___10. Eating disorders
___11. Self-mutilating
___12. Obsessively clean
___13. Drug and/or alcohol abuse
___14. Delinquent behavior
___15. Extreme compliance or defiance
___16. Fearful, anxious
___17. Suicidal gestures or attempts
___18. *Promiscuous or engaging in prostitution
___19. Engages in fantasy or infantile behavior
___20. Unwilling to participate in sports activities
___21. School difficulties
___22. Running away

Sexual Abuse—Physical Indicators:

___1. *Pain and/or itching in the genital area
___2. *Bruises or bleeding in the genital area
___3. *Venereal disease
___4. *Private parts are swollen
___5. *Difficulty walking or sitting
___6. *Torn, bloody, and/or stained underclothing
___7. Experiences pain when urinating
___8. *Pregnant
___9. *Vaginal or penile discharge
___10. Bedwetting

Emotional Abuse—Behavioral Indicators:

___1. Overanxious to please
___2. Seeks out adult contact
___3. Views abuse as warranted
___4. Changes in normal behavior
___5. Excessive anxiety
___6. Depression
___7. Unwillingness to discuss problems
___8. Aggressive or bizarre behavior
___9. Withdrawn
___10. Emotional apathy
___11. Passivity
___12. Unprovoked yelling or screaming
___13. Inconsistent behavior at home and school
___14. Feels responsible for the abuser
___15. Running away

___16. Suicide attempts
___17. Low self-esteem
___18. Gradual impairment of health and/or personality
___19. Difficulty sustaining relationships
___20. Unrealistic goal setting
___21. Impatient
___22. Inability to communicate or express feelings, needs, or desires
___23. Sabotages success
___24. Lack of self-confidence
___25. Self-deprecation and negative self-image

Emotional Abuse—Physical Indicators:

___1. Sleep disorders (nightmares, restlessness)
___2. Bedwetting
___3. Developmental lags (stunting of child's physical, emotional, and mental growth)
___4. Hyperactivity
___5. *Eating disorders

Physical Abuse—Behavioral Indicators:

___1. Wary of adults
___2. Either extremely aggressive or withdrawn
___3. Often clingy and indiscriminate with attachments
___4. Uncomfortable when other children cry
___5. Generally controls own crying
___6. Exhibits a drastic behavior change when not with parents or caregiver

___7. Manipulative

___8. Poor self-concept

___9. Delinquent behavior

___10. Drug or alcohol use

___11. Self-mutilation

___12. Frightened of parents or going home

___13. Overprotective of, or responsible for, parents

___14. Suicide attempts or gestures

___15. School behavior problems

___16. Running away

Physical Abuse—Physical Indicators:

___1. Unexplained* bruises or welts (often clustered or in a pattern)

___2. Unexplained* and/or unusual burns (cigarettes, donut-shaped, immersion lines, object patterned)

___3. Unexplained* bite marks

___4. Unexplained* fractures or dislocations

___5. Unexplained* abrasions or lacerations

___6. Bedwetting

(*or explanation is inconsistent or improbable)

Neglect—Behavioral Indicators

___1. Often truant or tardy to school, or arrives early and stays late

___2. Begs or steals food

___3. Suicidal gestures or attempts

___4. Uses or abuses alcohol or drugs

___5. Extremely clingy or detached

___6. Engages in delinquent behavior

___7. Appears exhausted

___8. States frequent or continual absence of parent or guardian

___9. Stealing

___10. Engages in prostitution

Neglect—Physical Indicators:

___1. Frequently dirty, unwashed, hungry, or inappropriately dressed

___2. Unsupervised and therefore engages in dangerous activities

___3. Tired,listless

___4. Has unattended physical problems

___5. May appear overworked or exploited

© Becca C. Johnson, PhD, 1992
For Their Sake: Recognizing, Reporting, and Responding to Child Abuse, ACA

APPENDIX B

Letter to the Abuser

*Note: For some, writing this letter has been helpful in the healing process, whether sent or burnt. Of course, you choose if you are ready and willing.**

To: _____,

    I've thought about writing or talking with you about this many times, but there are so many emotions. Even now as I write this, I am feeling _____ and

_____.

    I am _____ and _____ *(emotions)* at you for hurting me. If I could go back, with my current knowledge and understanding, I would tell you _____

_____

_____.

When the abuse was happening, I used to hope that you would _____

_____

_____.

After it happened, I wished you _____

_____

_____.

I used to think _____

_____

_____.

I've wanted to tell you _____

_____

_____

_____

_____

_____

_____

_____.

Signed: _____ Date: _____

P.S. _____

_____

Writing this letter is optional. Some have done this even though the person is dead or unknown. While some find this helpful, others find it too painful or irrelevant. Write this letter only when you feel ready (safe and strong) and have supportive friends, family, or a professional counselor to help you process all the thoughts and emotions. To give or to burn—discuss the pros and cons with your support people.

APPENDIX C

Letter to a Non-offending Caregiver*

Note: This letter can aid in the healing process, whether given or discarded.

To: _____ (Mom, dad, step-parent, non-offending caregiver)

I've thought about writing or talking with you about this many times, but there are so many emotions. Even now, as I write this, I am feeling _____ and _____.

I know I should be mad at the abuser, the one who hurt me, but all too often I feel anger at _____ for/because _____.

I've also felt _____ about _____.

When the abuse was happening, I used to dream that you would _____
_____.

After it happened, I wished you _____,
_____,

I used to wonder if _____
_____.

When you found out about what was happening/had happened to me, I was glad that you

_____
_____.

When you found out about what was happening/had happened to me, I was sad that you

_____
_____.

I also wish _____.

_____

Now that you know about the abuse, I'd also like you to know _____

_____
_____
_____
_____

Signed: _____ Date: _____

Writing this letter is optional. Some have done this even though the person is dead or unknown. While some find this helpful, others find it too painful or irrelevant. Do only when you feel ready (safe and strong) and have supportive friends, family, or a professional counselor to help you process all the thoughts and emotions. To give or to discard—discuss the pros and cons with your support people.

ENDNOTES

Chapter 1: The Journey to Hope?

Centers for Disease Control and Prevention, the ACE study.

Felitti, V. J., R. F. Anda, D. Nordenberg D, et al., "Relationship of childhood abuse and household dysfunction to many of the leading causes of death in adults: The Adverse Childhood Experiences (ACE) Study," *American Journal of Preventive Medicine* 14, no. 4 (1998): 245–258.

Anda, R. F., V. J. Felitti, J. D. Bremner JD, et al., "The enduring effects of abuse and related adverse experiences in childhood," European Archives of Psychiatry and Clinical Neuroscience 256, no. 3 (2006): 174–186.

Chapter 2: Understanding How Healing Happens

1 *Information on trauma treatment components:*

Pelcovitz, et al., "Development of a criteria set and a structured interview for disorders of extreme stress (SIDES)," *Journal of Traumatic Stress* 10, no. 1 (1997): 3–16

(ISTSS Expert Consensus, 2012)

Saunders, B. E., L. Berliner, and R. F. Hanson (Eds.), *Child Physical and Sexual Abuse: Guidelines for Treatment (Revised Report: April 26, 2004).* Charleston, SC:

National, Crime Victims Research and Treatment Center, 2004.

National Child Traumatic Stress Network, *Complex Trauma in Children and Adolescents.* National Child Traumatic Stress Network, 2008.

Courtois, Christine, PhD, Understanding Complex Trauma, Complex Reactions, and Treatment Approaches www.drchriscourtois.com, http://gift-fromwithin.org/html/cptsd-understanding-treat-ment.html.

Chapter 3: What is Abuse

Chapter 5 Who is Abused, How Much, and How Often

2 "Child Maltreatment 2012." Acf.hhs.gov. Last modi-fied December 17, 2013. http://www.acf.hhs.gov/programs/cb/resource/child-maltreatment-2012

3 "Child Abuse Statistics and Facts." Childhelp.org. http://www.childhelp.org/pages/statistics

4 *Adverse Childhood Experiences* conducted by the Center for Disease Control and Kaiser Permanente.

5 Allender, Dan, *Wounded Heart.* NavPress, 1994, 36.

6 Revictimization research: van der Kolk 1989; van der Kolk, Roth, Pelcovitz, Mandel, and Spinazzola, 2005; Yehuda, Spertus, and Golier, 2001.

Chapter 6: Who Abuses?

7 *Long-Term Consequences of Child Abuse and Neglect.* Child Welfare Information Gateway. Washington, DC: US Department of Health and Human Services: 2013. *http://www.childwelfare.gov/pubs/factsheets/long_term_consequences.cfm.*

8 Forward, Susan and Craig Buck. Penguin Books; Revised edition (September 1, 1988).

9 Child Maltreatment 2012. Children's Bureau: An Office of the Administration for Children and Families. December 17, 2013.
http://www.acf.hhs.gov/programs/cb/resource/child-maltreatment-2012.

10 *Advances in Clinical Child Psychology* http://www.victimsofcrime.org/media/reporting-on-child-sexual-abuse/statistics-on-perpetrators-of-csa.

Chapter 8: How Our Bodies React

11 Levine, Peter, *Waking the Tiger—Healing Trauma.* North Atlantic Books: 1997, 16, 86.

12 Levine, Peter, *Waking the Tiger—Healing Trauma.* North Atlantic Books: 1997, 95–96.

Chapter 11: Why We Keep Silent

13 Johnson, Rebecca C., PhD, "Aftercare for Survivors of Human Trafficking," *Social Work and Christianity: An International Journal,* 39, no. 4 (2012) NACSW: National Association of Christians in Social Work.

14 Jonzon and Lindblad, 2004; Smith et al., 2000; Wyatt, 1990.

15 Lyon, 2007; Malloy, Lyon, and Quas, 2007; Foynes, Freyd, and DePrince, 2009.

16 Schaeffer, Leventhal, and Asnes, *Barriers to Disclosure*, 2011.

17 Freyd, Jennifer J. University of Oregon, Copyright, Jennifer Freyd, 2010, Annual Convention of the American Psychological Association, 14 August 2010.

Chapter 12: How We Feel

18 Johnson, Rebecca C., PhD, "Aftercare for Survivors of Human Trafficking," *Social Work and Christianity: An International Journal*, 39, no. 4 (2012) NACSW: National Association of Christians in Social Work.

19 McCullough, Sandage, and Worthington, *To Forgive Is Human: How to Put Your Past in the Past*. InterVarsity Press, 1998, 190, 191, 196, 197.

20 Arterburn, Stephen, *Seven Keys to Spiritual Renewal*. Tyndale House, 1998.

Appendix A: Possible Abuse Indicators

21 Becca C. Johnson, PhD, *For Their Sake: Recognizing, Reporting, and Responding to Child Abuse*. ACA, 1992.

97726026R00139